Let's Start the MUSIC

The Urbana Free Library

To renew: call 217-367-4057
or go to "*urbanafreelibrary.org*"
and select "Renew/Request Items"

ALA Editions purchases fund advocacy, awareness, and accreditation programs for library professionals worldwide.

Let's Start the MUSIC

Programming
for Primary Grades

AMY BROWN

ala editions

An imprint of the American Library Association
Chicago | 2014

Amy Brown, who has worked in libraries for fourteen years, is currently a library manager for Worthington Libraries in Worthington, Ohio. She has presented at state and national conferences, taught workshops for libraries, and written articles on using music and the theory of multiple intelligences in children's programming. Amy has an MLIS degree from Wayne State University in Detroit, Michigan. This is her first book.

© 2014 by the American Library Association.

Excerpt from *Bedtime at the Swamp*, by Kristyn Crow, used by permission of HarperCollins Publishers.

Printed in the United States of America
18 17 16 15 14   5 4 3 2 1

ISBNs: 978-0-8389-1166-2 (paper); 978-0-8389-9692-8 (PDF). For more information on digital formats, visit the ALA Store at alastore.ala.org and select eEditions.

Library of Congress Cataloging-in-Publication Data

Brown, Amy, 1976-
  Let's start the music : programming for primary grades / Amy Brown.
      pages   cm
  Includes bibliographical references and index.
  ISBN 978-0-8389-1166-2
  1. Children's libraries—Activity programs—United States. 2. School
libraries—Activity programs—United States. 3. Music—Instruction and study—United States. I. Title.
  Z718.3.B76 2014
  027.62'5—dc23

                                                                    2013010871

Cover design by Casey Bayer. Image © Shutterstock, Inc.
Text design by Kirstin Krutsch in Snidley and Gentium Book Basic.

♾ This paper meets the requirements of ANSI/NISO Z39.48–1992 (Permanence of Paper).

To my mom, Cindy, who started me on
this magical musical journey

CONTENTS

ACKNOWLEDGMENTS

 would like to thank my family for their love and support and for helping me check out all those books and CDs from the library. Thank you, Mom, for sharing your many musical tips and classroom experiences with me. Megan, thank you for editing the manuscript (several times!) and for encouraging me through this whole process. Molly, thank you for introducing me to the theory of multiple intelligences and the wonders of programming with kazoos. Stephanie Zvirin, ALA acquisitions editor, thank you for giving me this amazing opportunity and for all of your help along the way.

INTRODUCTION

ne summer I shared with a group of first through third graders one of my all-time favorite stories, *Abiyoyo*, by Pete Seeger (Simon and Schuster Books for Young Readers, 2001). *Abiyoyo* is about a boy and his father who each has a talent that annoys the neighboring town. The boy plays his ukulele, and the father plays magical jokes on unsuspecting neighbors. When the townsfolk have had enough, they send the two away, only to realize later that they need their special talents when a huge, slobbery giant comes to town. This story has it all: magic, a giant, a child with a great big idea that saves the day, and a catchy song that kids can sing with enthusiasm.

Before reading the book, I taught children the song. Then, as I read the story, they had an opportunity to join in and sing it over and over. After the library program finished, a boy ran out to his mother and excitedly told her about the tale and singing the song. The mother told me how happy she was because she remembered both from her childhood and was thrilled to be able to check out the book and share that memory with her son.

Musical moments like this are special. Think back on some of your favorite musical memories. What song did you listen to over and over? What musical memory or experience is vivid for you? When I was growing up, my mom and siblings and I would dance in the kitchen to Carole King while making dinner. I remember my first job, hoeing a massive field of beans (I grew up on a farm), and then using my paycheck to buy a radio. That began my love affair with the radio station CK 105.5. I remember my last piano recital and the hardest piece I've every played, Rachmaninoff's Prelude in C Sharp Minor. The boys I took piano lessons with often got the fast, loud, and fun recital pieces, but not that time.

Musical experiences can be memory making and magical, and that's why I love sharing music with children. It's thrilling to see kids excitedly sharing songs they've learned in a program or to hear a boy say that he can't wait for the next library event because he's going to make a shoe-box guitar. I love it when I listen to a new children's song and know just the group to share it with. I enjoy watching kids play with instruments they've never seen and try to figure out how they work. Music has power. It's social, it's creative, it's play, it's improvising, and it's learning. It's not just singing in tune, taking piano lessons, or having innate talent. Music is for everybody, and it connects with each of us in unique ways. Sometimes, as adults, we forget the joy of music, the thrill of creating, and the enjoyment of sharing that experience with others. It becomes easy to say, "I can't sing," or "I'm too old to learn how to play an instrument."

My hope is that this book will provide entertaining, easy-to-implement ideas, and helpful resources for using music with children in primary grades. You don't have to know how to play an instrument or need to be able to sing in tune. Trust me, I do not have a perfectly in-tune voice. I often joke that I can tell when I'm not singing in tune, but that doesn't mean I can fix the situation! I also don't play a guitar or the piano in my programs, although many people do. That's OK. Children don't care about whether you have a good voice. They don't care if you mess up on a rhythm or do the wrong steps in a line dance. Those mistakes make it easier for them to experiment, to try new things, and to not worry about having to be perfect. They just want to play and have fun. That's all they want from you, too.

I believe in the following musical premises and have written this book based on them:

▶ We all have musical talent.
▶ There are many ways to be musical.
▶ We can grow in our musical ability.
▶ Music has powerful benefits in our lives.
▶ Music is meant to be shared.
▶ The library is a great place to experience and experiment with music.

In this book you will find information about the importance of using music with children; ways to introduce children to songs and instruments; thirteen ready-made thematic program plans; an appendix of action songs and an appendix with a cross-reference of additional themed resources.

The thematic programs are designed to be used with children in kindergarten through third grade. Each theme starts with an outline ("playlist") for an hour-long program that is composed of books, songs, an activity, and an opportunity for making and using musical instruments like kazoos, guitars, drums, and shakers. My philosophy is to always overplan for a program. I never know how many kids I'm going to have, what the majority age is going to be, or how they will respond to the material that I've prepared. Sometimes a book or song will take much longer to share because the crowd is interacting with the material and really responding to it. Sometimes four books will be too much for an active group, and most of the program ends up being songs and activities. Other times the group wants more stories. I have a plan and flow for the program, but in the moment, I tailor it to each group. You may find that a playlist has too many songs or that you don't have time to do the activity and the musical instrument. Please adjust the material to your group and programming style.

I start my programs by introducing the theme. To do this, I share some information about the topic and ask the group questions. For example, in the theme that looks at sound, I have children close their eyes and listen to a sound. Then I ask them to guess what makes that sound. Sometimes I share facts, riddles, or realia relating to the theme. After introducing the theme, I start with a song and alternate between reading stories and sharing songs for thirty to forty minutes.

I like to have an activity or game in each program. Sometimes I'll do the activity at the beginning, giving the group something to work on while we wait for latecomers to arrive. Other times I use it to transition to the instrument craft. I finish the program with children working together to design their own instrument. During this time, I play music in the background. For kids who finish early, I have books for them to look at and a collection of musical instruments they can explore.

Everyone has unique programming styles and what works for one person may not work for another. For that reason, I've included "bonus books" and "bonus tracks" for each theme. These are additional mix-and-match options so that you can pick and choose material that is most comfortable for you. There is enough material for additional programs on the same theme or variants of the theme.

My hope is that this book will help you discover new tales, entertaining songs, and interactive activities that will assist you in creating musical memories with children.

Let the music making begin!

CHAPTER 1
THE IMPORTANCE
OF MUSIC

en years ago a librarian friend of mine introduced me to Howard Gardner's theory of multiple intelligences (MI theory), and I began rethinking how I use music in library programming. I embarked on a reading journey that changed how I looked at the process of learning; what it means to be smart; and how to make library programming appealing to a variety of children, not just those who naturally gravitate toward books and reading.

MULTIPLE INTELLIGENCES: WHAT ARE THEY?

Howard Gardner developed the theory of multiple intelligences in the early 1980s. The theory is based on the belief that intelligence is more intricate and varied than people sometimes realize. A score on an IQ test doesn't tell the whole story about people and their intelligence. Gardner writes, "I believe that human cognitive competence is better described in terms of a set of abilities, talents, or mental skills, which I call *intelligences*."[1] There are eight intelligences: linguistic, logical-mathematical, musical, spatial, bodily-kinesthetic, interpersonal, intrapersonal, and naturalist.

The theory of multiple intelligences has the following premises:

▶ Everyone has eight intelligences, but not everyone has the same skill level for each intelligence. For example, an artist may be very strong in the bodily-kinesthetic and spatial intelligences but not as strong in the logical-mathematical intelligence.

▶ Each intelligence is multifaceted. There's more than one way to demonstrate an aptitude for an intelligence. For example, with musical intelligence one person may be a proficient pianist while another writes emotional lyrics and yet another selects the perfect song to be played during a pivotal movie scene.

▶ The intelligences aren't static (this is one of my favorite premises). We can improve upon them. Although I grew up on a farm, I am not strong in the naturalist intelligence. That doesn't mean that I'm hopeless or that I can't grow in that intelligence with time and work.

▶ Intelligences are not exclusive of each other. They mix together in amazing and intricate ways. Imagine yourself as a surgeon. You may use music to help you focus on the task or to keep you relaxed through the hours of grueling surgery. You use your interpersonal skills to communicate with the people on your surgical team. You use your spatial skills to visualize what needs to happen during the surgery, and you use the bodily-kinesthetic intelligence to execute the intricate movements required for a successful surgery.[2]

THE EIGHT INTELLIGENCES

This section includes a brief synopsis of each of the intelligences. I have included MI theory resources at the end of the section for further study.

Linguistic intelligence: Linguistic people have an affinity for language and working with language. They can do this through the written word, through storytelling, or through giving speeches. A child who is strong in this intelligence might enjoy a book like *Rip the Page! Adventures in Creative Writing*, by Karen Benke (Trumpeter, 2010). Or he or she might want to try some of the suggested activities, like keeping a favorite word list or creating spoonerisms.

Logical-mathematical: Logical-mathematical people may be strong in logic, math, and science. They may enjoy puzzles, word problems, and science experiments. Kids who are strong in this intelligence often like nonfiction books that explain how and why. They might like a book like *Cool Special Effects: How to Stage Your Very Own Show*, by Karen Latchana Kenney (ABDO Publishing, 2010), which might appeal to them because it explains the science behind light and sound effects.

Musical: Musical people may play instruments, hear rhythms, notice what is out of tune, write their own music, or critique the music of others. They may like to sing, compose pieces, craft playlists for special events, or participate in a band. They might read a book like *Learn to Speak Music: A Guide to Creating, Performing, and Promoting Your Songs*, by John Crossingham and illustrated by Jeff Kulak (Owlkids Books, 2009). Then they might use what they learn to help them decide what instrument to play and how to write a song.

Spatial: Spatial people use their visual abilities to help them learn and process information. They may express themselves in images. Sketching, photography, and design are activities they may gravitate toward. They might like to do crayon scratchboard creations or eraser art from the book *Art Lab for Kids: 52 Creative Adventures in Drawing, Painting, Printmaking, Paper, and Mixed Media*, by Susan Schwake (Quarry Books, 2012).

Bodily-kinesthetic: Bodily-kinesthetic people use their body to learn, to create, and to communicate. They may have coordination and precision of movement. They might enjoy sports, dance, physical comedy, and building or making things. They might learn choreography and various dance styles from books like *Learn to Speak Dance: A Guide to Creating, Performing, and Promoting Your Moves*, by Ann-Marie Williams and illustrated by Jeff Kulak (Owlkids Books, 2011).

Interpersonal: Interpersonal people know how to read a crowd and communicate to a group. They may enjoy working in teams, leading a group or activity, or teaching others how to do something. They might want to plan a block party to help neighbors get to know one another or create a cleanup day for the neighborhood. They might learn how to do these things by reading a book like *Ways to Help in Your Community*, by Claire O'Neal (Mitchell Lane Publishers, 2011).

Intrapersonal: Intrapersonal people seek to understand themselves better. They are honest about their strengths and weaknesses and may like to take personality quizzes or spend time in self-reflection. They may enjoy reading a book like *You're Smarter Than You Think: A Kid's Guide to Multiple Intelligences*, by Thomas Armstrong (Free Spirit Publishing, 2003). The book has quizzes they can take to see what intelligences they are strong in. It also has suggestions for activities they can do to improve their intelligence in different areas.

Naturalist: Naturalist people pay close attention to their environment. They may like to explore nature or classify things in their neighborhood, like the different architectural elements that can be found on a city street. A child who is strong in the naturalist intelligence might enjoy growing carrots or sweet potatoes in the kitchen or planting a pizza garden. These activities and more can be found in the book *The Budding Gardener*, edited by Mary B. Rein and illustrated by Jane Dippold (Gryphon House, 2011).[3]

The following books have additional information about MI theory:

Armstrong, Thomas. *Multiple Intelligences in the Classroom*. 3rd ed. Alexandria, VA: ASCD, 2009.

Gardner, Howard. *Frames of Mind: The Theory of Multiple Intelligences*. 3rd ed. New York: Basic Books, 2011.

———. *Multiple Intelligences: New Horizons*. New York: Basic Books, 2006.

LIBRARY PROGRAMMING WITH MI THEORY

When I started programming using MI theory, I began to look at music differently. Music became more than playing a song on a CD that fit with the theme of the day. I explored new ways for children to interact with music and ways to use music to interact with the other intelligences.

For each of the programs in this book, I include a variety of ways to connect with music, and I incorporate at least several of the intelligences. Some of the techniques that I use are the following:

- ▶ Asking questions to help children relate the theme to themselves and to others (intrapersonal and interpersonal)
- ▶ Including movement activities like playing instruments, engaging in games, or participating in action songs (bodily-kinesthetic)
- ▶ Highlighting nonfiction books that have facts, puzzles, jokes, or science experiments that connect to the theme (logical-mathematical)
- ▶ Bringing in musical instruments for children to look at and play (spatial and bodily-kinesthetic)
- ▶ Using natural or recycled elements for instruments and sharing books that feature nature (naturalist)

Music and Early Literacy

Not only is music an important part of MI theory; it is also a vital part of early literacy. In the summer of 2011, the Public Library Association and Association for Library Service to Children rolled out the second edition of the toolkit Every Child Ready to Read® @ your library®, an update to the early literacy initiative Every Child Ready to Read. The new framework has five practices that parents and caregivers can do with their children to help them develop early literacy skills. One of those practices is singing, and music helps children develop early literacy skills in a couple of ways.

Let's look at the song "Old MacDonald Had a Farm." When we sing the song, we sing the words slower than we would say them, allowing children to hear the individual words. Also, in many songs the syllables of words are associated with different musical notes. This is an auditory clue that helps children realize that words are made up of different sounds. Both of these musical traits assist with phonological awareness.

Just like picture books, songs use words and describe objects that children might not be familiar with. If you sing "Old MacDonald" and include a variety of different animals, like goats, llamas, chickens, and rabbits, children who don't live on a farm and aren't familiar with farmers can learn about them. This increases their vocabulary.

Singing songs like "Old MacDonald Had a Farm" are enjoyable for young children because they can make the animal sounds and help develop additional verses. They participate in the creation of music while at the same time having fun with language. This assists with print motivation. For more information about the five practices, check out Every Child Ready to Read®, Second Edition Kit (ALSC and PLA, 2011).

Additional Benefits of Music

Music is social and can be used to create community. We play music during many types of family and community events, such as birthdays, weddings, and graduations. Playing musical instruments in a band or a class requires that musicians work together to create music. Bobby McFerrin once said, "The most wonderful thing about music is that it's not really meant to be kept close to the breast, as they say. You know it's not for yourself alone. I think music is something to be shared with people."[4] In the library or classroom setting, learning songs together, playing musical games, and creating music are all social activities.

Music can also be used to elicit emotion. When we want to feel a certain way, we might pick music that will help us experience that emotion. People exercise to upbeat, energetic music. Moviemakers create soundtracks to emphasize the emotion in pivotal scenes. Music played during children's library programming can also set the tone. A quiet interlude may calm a crowd. An energetic, silly song may cause laughter.

Music inspires movement. It's very hard to listen to music and not move. Nodding the head, swaying from side to side, snapping fingers, clapping hands, and tapping toes are all natural responses to music. Including action songs in programs can help refocus a restless audience or add an enjoyable interactive element.

Music helps with memory. Some teachers use rap music to help their students remember math and science concepts. A song about space might help kids learn and remember the names of the planets months later. A song about the Dewey decimal system can help children remember where to find science books or fairy tales. Throughout history music has been used to tell stories. People have passed down traditional songs from generation to generation to share important information.

Music also inspires creativity, improvisation, and play, and we can find examples of this innovation throughout the ages. Instruments and musical genres change over time as people and cultures interact with them. The amazing thing about music is that we all have the opportunity to be a part of the music conversation and create our own musical story.

NOTES

1. Howard Gardner, *Multiple Intelligences: New Horizons* (New York: Basic Books, 2006), 6.
2. Thomas Armstrong, *Multiple Intelligences in the Classroom*, 3rd edition (Alexandria, VA: ASCD, 2009), 15–16.
3. Thomas Armstrong, *You're Smarter Than You Think: A Kid's Guide to Multiple Intelligences* (Minneapolis: Free Spirit, 2003), 3–4.
4. Elena Mannes, *The Power of Music: Pioneering Discoveries in the New Science of Song* (New York: Walker & Company, 2011), 212.

CHAPTER 2
INCORPORATING SONGS AND INSTRUMENTS INTO LIBRARY PROGRAMMING

s a children's librarian I have played many musical recordings with children, mostly during storytimes, but I didn't always use music in school-age programming. I didn't know how to teach children to sing a song, and I didn't use musical instruments (beyond egg shakers) in my programs. When I started experimenting with musical activities, I witnessed children collaborating and engaging in conversations about making instruments out of recycled materials. I saw the wonder of a child picking up a shekere, a hollow gourd covered with a net of beads, and exploring how it makes musical sounds. I watched how music helps children leave library programs with something new that they've learned and that they enjoy sharing with their family and friends. Music making shouldn't stop at storytimes or when children enter school. Music making is even more fun with school-age children because you can explore musical concepts in more depth than you can with younger children.

This chapter provides an overview of ways to use music with children by teaching them songs and by using handmade or purchased instruments in programming. Cindy Brown, a retired elementary and music teacher, and the woman who inspired my love of music, assisted with the chapter, sharing tips and suggestions she's gathered from working with children for more than thirty-five years.

PICKING THE RIGHT SONG

What is the best way to find music to use in your program? Start with what you know. Take a musical inventory of yourself and your coworkers. What were your favorite songs growing up? What lullabies do you remember? What songs did you learn in school or at camp? A memorable song for my friends and me is "I'm Just a Bill" from *Schoolhouse Rock*. Look at the list of music that you've compiled. Can you use any of these songs or melodies in your library programming? With so many songs to choose from, it can be hard to decide which songs to use. Here are a few suggestions that I keep in mind when I'm picking out music:

- ▶ The first and most important thing is, do I like the song? If it's not fun for me, it's not going to be pleasurable to teach, and it won't be enjoyable for children to learn. It may fit my theme or be on the right topic, but if it doesn't connect with me, it won't connect with my audience either.
- ▶ Is the topic interesting or relatable to children? Is it humorous? I love using silly songs with children.
- ▶ Does it include movement in the song, or can I add actions to it? I often alternate between reading a story and sharing a song in my programming. It's really hard for kids to sit for a long time, so songs with associated actions help kids release restless energy and help refocus the group before the next story.
- ▶ Does the song have repetition? Repeated words, phrases, and melodies help children learn and remember the song.
- ▶ Can the song be extended with additional verses? Children enjoy creating their own lyrics to songs.
- ▶ Does the song have an interesting musical accompaniment, or does it introduce children to another style of music?
- ▶ Last, will the song be too long, too complicated, too fast, or too high in vocal range for children to sing?

Traditional Songs

Some of the songs that you may remember as favorites probably are considered traditional songs. Traditional songs or folk songs have been around for a long time and often have been passed down from generation to generation. They usually aren't attributed to one particular person. They tend to have repetition to help people remember and share the song.

Camps use a lot of traditional songs, so if you have attended camp or worked at a camp, you probably know some great songs to use. Camp songs are often funny and usually have actions associated with the words. Some of my favorites are "Bananas," "Alice the Camel," and "My Bonnie." Traditional songs are great because people are often familiar with the music and words, which makes the songs easier to learn and share. Here are a few resources to help find traditional songs:

- ▶ Ladybug Music (http://ladybugmusic.com) has a majority of traditional music and a variety of musical styles in its recordings. The music is used in Ladybug Music Classes designed for the four-and-younger set, but I think some of the songs also work really well with older kids.
- ▶ The National Institute of Environmental Health Sciences (http://kids.niehs.nih.gov/games/songs/index.htm) has a kids' section on its website where you can find a selection of children's songs with both lyrics and audio files.
- ▶ *The Neighborhood Sing-Along*, by Nina Crews (Greenwillow Books, 2011). Crews has collected a variety of nursery rhymes and public-domain songs, including "John Jacob Jingleheimer Schmidt," "Miss Mary Mack," and "There's a Hole in the Bucket."
- ▶ Smithsonian Folkways (www.folkways.si.edu/explore _folkways/children.aspx) has a section on its website that highlights folk music for children. The site includes some sound files of music that can be found on the recordings that they sell. There is also a section titled "Tools for Teaching" that contains lesson plans and activities to use with folk songs.
- ▶ *The Super Songbook for Kids* (Amsco Publications, 2007). In this book thirty-seven traditional songs are arranged for piano, voice, and guitar. "This Old Man," "Do Your Ears Hang Low?" "Five Little Monkeys," "Who Stole the Cookie from the Cookie Jar?" and "On Top of Old Smoky" are a few of the songs.
- ▶ Wee Sing (www.weesing.com) has a series of books and CDs that feature traditional songs. A few that would be good to use with school-age children include *Wee Sing Fun 'n' Folk*, *Wee Sing around the World*, and *Wee Sing Games, Games, Games*.

Contemporary Songs

The world of children's music is varied and diverse. There are a lot of children's musicians out there who perform in a variety of musical styles. You can find a song on almost anything, from how the heart works, to finding monsters in the closet, to the blues of losing a tennis shoe. When picking songs to feature in this book, I looked for interesting musical and vocal arrangements and engaging and appealing lyrics. The songs I use in the program plans aren't too long, and they usually have a movement component and repetition. Some of the songs in the "Bonus Tracks" section are longer and may be better suited for background music during craft time or before the program starts.

Here are some review sources and publishers to help you find contemporary children's music:

- ▶ The American Library Association's Notable Children's Recordings Committee (www.ala.org/alsc/awardsgrants/notalists) publishes a list of notable recordings every year that includes some music CDs.
- ▶ CD Baby (www.cdbaby.com) is an online independent music store that sells a variety of music, including music for kids and families.
- ▶ Kimbo Educational (www.kimboed.com) has CDs that focus on educational topics like literacy, science, and fitness.
- ▶ Putumayo Kids (www.putumayo.com/kids/home) offers CDs featuring music from around the world on topics like rock and roll, jazz, and party music.
- ▶ School Library Journal (www.schoollibraryjournal.com) reviews sound recordings.
- ▶ Digital music sites like Spotify (www.spotify.com/us) or Pandora (www.pandora.com) suggest music for you on the basis of the artists and songs you like.

Creating Your Own Song

Sometimes it's fun to create your own song or to include the audience in song writing. One way to do this is to take traditional songs with tunes many people recognize and then update the lyrics. Here are a few suggestions to help craft songs for whatever program theme you have:

- ▶ Brainstorm words that describe the theme.
- ▶ Select a traditional song that would be easy to adapt. Think about tunes that have lots of repetition, like the following:
  - ▶ "Bingo"
  - ▶ "If You're Happy and You Know It"
  - ▶ "Old MacDonald Had a Farm"
  - ▶ "The Wheels on the Bus"
- ▶ Look for tunes with comfortable melodies. It makes it easier to sing songs with new words if you are already familiar with the music. Some examples are the following:
  - ▶ "Baa, Baa, Black Sheep"
  - ▶ "Head, Shoulders, Knees, and Toes"
  - ▶ "Itsy Bitsy Spider"
  - ▶ "London Bridge Is Falling Down"
  - ▶ "The More We Get Together"
  - ▶ "My Bonnie Lies over the Ocean"
  - ▶ "Skip to My Lou"
  - ▶ "Twinkle, Twinkle, Little Star"
- ▶ Look at the structure of the traditional song and play around with substitutions. For example:
  - ▶ The song "Bingo" can be changed to feature any word with five letters.

    "G-H-O-S-T"
    There was a house that had a haunting
    And Ghost was his name-o
    G-H-O-S-T
    G-H-O-S-T
    G-H-O-S-T
    And Ghost was his name-o

▶ Use the action song "Head, Shoulders, Knees, and Toes" for any topic or object that has three or four parts or sections:

> "Petals, Leaves, Stems, and Roots"
> Petals, leaves, stems, and roots, stems and roots.
> Petals, leaves, stems, and roots, stems and roots.
> Tulips, daisies, lilies, and roses.
> Petals, leaves, stems, and roots, stems and roots.

This same tune is used to teach children the parts of an insect in the song "Head Thorax Abdomen" from the recording *Boogie Woogie Bugs*, by Johnette Downing (Wiggle Worm Records, 2010).

▶ The Scottish folk song "Aiken Drum" features a man who lives in the moon and whose different pieces of clothing and body parts are made of food. You can switch this to a person who is made up of something else like nature objects or sports equipment or even musical instruments.

> "Conductor Bob"
> There was a musician who loved to play music, loved to play music,
>   loved to play music.
> There was a musician who loved to play music,
> And his name was Conductor Bob.
> His body was made of a cello, a cello, a cello.
> His body was made of a cello, and his name was Conductor Bob.
> Additional verses:
> His eyes were made of cymbals.
> His ears were made of castanets.
> His teeth were made of piano keys.
> His arms were made of trumpets.

For more samples and suggestions, check out the following:

Our Abe Lincoln, by Jim Aylesworth and illustrated by Barbara McClintock (Scholastic Press, 2009).
A Lincoln campaign song was written to the tune of the old folk song "The Old Gray Mare." Aylesworth takes that song and expands it to help children learn biographical facts about Abe Lincoln.

Rufus and Friends: School Days, by Iza Trapani (Charlesbridge, 2010).
In this collection about Ms. Schnickle's class of doggy students, Trapani takes fourteen traditional rhymes and extends them to focus on the school theme. A few fun ones to use include "The Ants Go Marching," about students filing into school at the start of the day, and "If You're Happy and You Know It, Clap Your Hands," with verses about learning, inquisitiveness, and enjoying school.

Smelly Locker: Silly Dilly School Songs, by Alan Katz and illustrated by David Catrow (Margaret K. McElderry Books, 2008).
Alan Katz has nine "silly dilly" songs with fresh and funny lyrics set to traditional tunes. For example, "Smelly Locker," a song about a gross, stinky locker, is sung to the tune of "Frère Jacques." Another song, "Tomorrow Is Our Class Picture Day," admonishes a person to act appropriately when getting his picture taken. This song is sung to the tune "When Johnny Comes Marching Home."

TEACHING CHILDREN A NEW SONG

Now that you have your song, what is the best way to introduce it to children? To illustrate the tips, I'll use three traditional songs: "The Bear Went over the Mountain," "Row, Row, Row Your Boat," and "My Bonnie."

"The Bear Went over the Mountain"
The bear went over the mountain.
The bear went over the mountain.
The bear went over the mountain,
To see what he could see.
And all that he could see,
And all that he could see,
Was the other side of the mountain,
The other side of the mountain.
The other side of the mountain,
Was all that he could see.

"Row, Row, Row Your Boat"
Row, row, row your boat
Gently down the stream.
Merrily, merrily,
Merrily, merrily,
Life is but a dream.

"My Bonnie"
My Bonnie lies over the ocean.
My Bonnie lies over the sea.
My Bonnie lies over the ocean.
So bring back my Bonnie to me.

Bring back, bring back,
Bring back my Bonnie to me, to me.
Bring back, bring back,
Bring back my Bonnie to me.

Introduce the song by posing a question relating to the song. For example, "This song has an animal in it. Listen to discover what kind of animal it is." Or "In this song, a bear goes over the mountain. Why do you think he does that?" After a little discussion, sing the song and let children provide the answer.

Another way to introduce the song is to share a little bit of history surrounding the song and to help children relate to it. For example: "'My Bonnie' is a folk song from Scotland. Where on this globe would you find Scotland?" or "'My Bonnie' is a song often sung at camp. Have any of you sung this song at camp?"

Melody

Instead of jumping right in and teaching the words to a song, have kids become familiar with the tune by humming it. You could also have them sing it with sounds like "la, la, la" or "do, do, do." Try singing "Row, Row, Row Your Boat" this way.

Lyrics

First, sing or play the song once so that children can hear the whole piece. If a song has repeated words or phrases, ask children to listen closely and count the number of times they hear a certain word or phrase. For example, ask children to count the number of times they hear the words *bear* or *mountain* in "The Bear Went Over the Mountain." After finishing the song, have children respond with their answer. If there is more than one "answer" being offered, say, "Hmmm, let's see if we can count it again," and then sing it again. This exercise helps children really focus on the words in the song.

After counting the words and singing the song several times, ask children to do a movement when they hear that same word or phrase. For example, say something like, "When I sing it this time, nod your head when you hear the word *bear*." You could also have children freeze when they hear the word. The movement you choose depends on the age of the children—use your judgment and be as creative as you dare, but know that eventually you'll need to regain their attention to continue teaching the song.

Another way to teach children the words of a song is to sing the song and let them fill in the blank. For "My Bonnie," sing, "My _____ lies over the ocean. My _____ lies over the sea." Or "My Bonnie lies over the _____. My Bonnie lies over the _____."

You can also divide children into two groups and have one group sing one phrase and a second group sing the other phrase. With "Row, Row, Row Your Boat," the first group sings "row, row, row your boat," and the second group sings "gently down the stream." You can also add a movement to the words so that every time the children hear the appropriate word, they pretend to row the boat with their hands or move their hands up and down to mimic the stream. Sing it again, and switch the word assignment. This time, have the children who were singing "row, row, row your boat" sing "gently down the stream."

Echoing is another way to teach a song. With this technique you sing a line, and children echo it back to you. With "Row, Row, Row Your Boat," you would sing, "Row, row, row your boat," and the group would echo it back. Then you would sing, "Gently down the stream," and again the audience would repeat the phrase.

Last, if the song has a story to it, consider having children act out the song. This produces a mind-body connection that will help them with memorization.

PUTTING EVERYTHING TOGETHER

Once you feel that children know enough of the song, ask them to sing as much of the song as they feel comfortable with. Invite them to join in by saying, "Sing with me if you're ready. If you're not, that's OK. Listen along with us." Some children don't feel comfortable singing in front of others or don't want to join the group. Giving them a "pass" to sit it out helps them still be a part of the group and provides them with an opportunity to try the song when they do feel ready.

Once the whole group is singing the song, one of my favorite activities is to have the group practice the song using different voices. Sing it high or low. Sing it fast or slow. Whisper it or shout it. Sing it like a country singer or an opera singer. The practice helps children learn and remember the song, but the silliness of the different voices makes the repetition fun and not boring.

Do I do every one of these techniques with every song I use in a program? No. There's not enough time in a library program for that, but I do pick and choose different techniques and use them with songs that I want children to remember. I'll use these techniques with a short song in a picture book, an opening song that we will sing for several weeks, or a song that conveys information that I want them to remember (like a song for a summer reading club).

DEVELOPING YOUR TECHNIQUE

The following are some examples of songs that use a few of the techniques mentioned.

"Boom Chicka Boom," from the recording *Let's Go! Travel, Camp and Car Songs*, by Susie Tallman and Friends (Rock Me Baby Records, 2007).
Tallman has listeners sing the song using various voices like a cowboy and jazz voice.

"Fried Ham," from the book and CD *Lisa Loeb's Silly Sing-Along: The Disappointing Pancake and Other Zany Songs*, by Lisa Loeb and illustrated by Ryan O'Rourke (Sterling Children's Books, 2011).
Loeb repeats the lyrics for "Fried Ham" several times with varying voices, including an opera voice and an underwater voice.

"No More Pie," from the recording *Play Your Instruments and Make a Pretty Sound*, by Ella Jenkins (Smithsonian/Folkways Records, 1994).
The first time Jenkins sings the song, she asks children to echo each line after her. The second time she leaves out key words that children should fill in, and the third time she sings every other line and has listeners

respond with the missing line. The end of each line rhymes, which helps with learning the song. At first it's hard to remember everything. Don't worry, though. Part of the fun is finding out what people remember or discovering the new verses people make up because they can't remember the real words. After singing the song through a couple of times, you'll be surprised how much you really do remember.

PICKING THE RIGHT INSTRUMENT

Kids enjoy playing musical instruments, and with a little bit of planning and not a lot of money, you can add music accompaniment to stories and songs in your programs.

There are a variety of simple instruments to use with children. Percussion instruments are probably the most common. Egg shakers, rhythm sticks, jingle-bell wristlets, or sand blocks might be instruments you already have and use in storytimes. These same instruments can be used with school-age kids.

I've had a lot of fun using kazoos with kids in programming. Kazoos can be purchased in bulk at party-supply stores and usually aren't too expensive. Music stores sometimes have inexpensive instruments like recorders and slide whistles. Fair-trade stores like Ten Thousand Villages often carry rattles, chimes, drums, and ocarinas. Dollar stores, toy stores, and toy sections of chain stores may have percussion instruments, harmonicas, and recorders.

If you are looking for a wide variety of instruments or for a large amount of one particular instrument, several online stores have options:

▶ Lakeshore Learning (www.lakeshorelearning.com)
▶ Music in Motion (www.musicmotion.com)

MAKING YOUR OWN INSTRUMENTS

Many musical instruments can be made from found or recyclable materials. In this book you will find instructions to make a series of instruments, like kazoos, tambourines, drums, and shakers. For some of the instruments, you will use materials found around the house: empty water bottles, paper-towel tubes, coffee containers, dried beans, and paper plates. Some of the instruments may require purchased materials like foam or jingle bells, but the cost is still less than purchasing instruments. You will also find information on how to play the spoons, use kitchen objects as instruments, and make music with rhythm sticks or unsharpened pencils.

You don't even have to buy or make prescribed instruments. For example, Stomp is a group of percussionists who create musical theater with everyday objects like brooms, newspapers, buckets, and their bodies. For inspiration, you can view a few Stomp video clips from the group's website (www.stomponline .com). I can't always bring musical instruments to an auditorium of students, but I can have them keep rhythm on their knees or make different sounds by snapping their fingers, clapping their hands, tapping their feet, or rubbing their hands together. One example of using your body as an instrument involves a large group creating the sounds of a rainstorm. If you look up "rainstorm choir" on YouTube, you can find a variety of videos of different choirs creating the sound of a rainstorm with their fingers, hands, and feet. Another musician who uses his body as an instrument is Bobby McFerrin. YouTube also has many videos highlighting Bobby McFerrin's work.

Rules for Instruments

Before passing out instruments, establish rules for musical play. Once children have their instruments, if they don't know the rules, it can be hard to rein in the group. Here are my basic rules:

- ▶ *Respect the instrument.* Introduce this concept by asking some questions: "What is this instrument that I'm holding? How do you think you make music with it?" Then say something like, "It's a lot of fun to play with instruments, but we have to be careful with them because they belong to the library. We want to be able to use them again and again."
- ▶ *Respect the conductor.* "What does a conductor do? What does a conductor use to direct a group of musicians?" Children might say that a conductor uses his or her hands, a baton, or a stick. You are the conductor, and you can use whatever you want to direct the children. The key is to have several movements associated with meanings so that children know when to be loud or quiet and when to play or stop playing. For example, you can use a conductor's baton and raise it high in the air to indicate that it's time to play loudly or bring it low to the ground to encourage children to play softly. You can tell children that when you point to them, it is their turn to play. When you point at yourself, it's time for them to stop. I don't

use a baton. I prefer to use my hands to make the motions. It's really up to you. The important thing is to have visual cues for children to direct them and bring them back when you need them to stop playing.

▶ *Respect other musicians.* Ask children, "Are you a musician?" Some will say yes, and some will say no. You can say, "We are all musicians today, and we are all going to play music. I want to hear each and every one of you, so it's important that we listen to what our neighbor is doing and not play so loudly we can't hear each other make music."

Different Ways to Use Instruments
Keep the Beat

Percussion instruments like shakers and rhythm sticks are great for keeping a beat. You can use them with chants, short poems, limericks, nursery rhymes, and songs. Here are some things you can do with shakers and rhythm sticks:

▶ Pick a nursery rhyme like "Jack and Jill," and chant the rhyme while children keep the beat by tapping their rhythm sticks or shaking an egg shaker or maraca.

▶ With the song "I Know a Chicken," from the recording *The Best of the Laurie Berkner Band*, by the Laurie Berkner Band (Two Tomatoes Records, 2010), break out the egg shakers and practice tempo. Berkner tells children when to shake them fast or slow.

▶ In the song "Stop and Go," from the recording *Play Your Instruments and Make a Pretty Sound*, by Ella Jenkins (Smithsonian/Folkways Records, 1994), children have to listen to the instructions so that they know when it is time to stop and go. Some of the actions include walking, skipping, and tapping knees. If you feel comfortable after learning the song, you can adapt it and sing it yourself to teach children how to play their instrument for a bit and then stop. One verse could be tapping a drum, and another could be shaking maracas.

▶ If you need a good rhythmic song for children to play their percussion instruments to, "Ratty Tat Tat," from the recording *There's a Train . . .*, by We Kids Rock! (We Kids Rock, 2009) is a great one. The band uses shakers throughout the song, and different animals take sticks and practice playing them. Children can tap along with rhythm sticks, or they can pat the rhythm on their knees.

▶ With "Two Little Blackbirds," from the recording *Ladybug Music: Yellow Collection*, by Ladybug Music (Ladybug Music, 2010), clap or use rhythm sticks to tap along to the rhythm of the song.

You can also use shakers and rhythm sticks with stories that have a steady rhythmic narration or that have repeated lines or chants. Here are a few examples of stories that illustrate that concept:

Bedtime at the Swamp, by Kristyn Crow and illustrated by Macky Pamintuan (HarperCollins, 2008).
Crow includes a chant that is repeated throughout the story. Use rhythm instruments to establish a pattern with the chant.

Brown Bear, Brown Bear, What Do You See? by Bill Martin Jr. and illustrated by Eric Carle (H. Holt, 1992).
For this story you can have children use rhythm sticks or tap their knees. They can do the same action through the whole story, or you can teach them a rhythm pattern—like tap, tap, clap, clap, tap, tap, clap, clap—and have them tap their knees or clap their hands. You can have them take the rhythm sticks and tap the floor or clap them together.

Represent Story Characters

Instruments can be used to represent characters. You can play the instrument when you are telling the story, or you can cue children to play certain instruments when different characters speak. If you are having children participate in the storytelling, work out a process whereby you cue children with your hand, with a nod of your head, or by saying certain words so that they know when it is their turn to play. A few story examples include the following:

The First Music, by Dylan Pritchett and illustrated by Erin Bennett Banks (August House Little Folk, 2006).
What transforms ordinary animal sounds into music? African animals go about their day until they discover the unique and special sounds that are

made through accidents like an elephant bumping into a log and creating a great booming sound. One animal after another uncovers a magical musical sound that when combined with the others creates the first music. Throughout the story, each animal produces a musical sound that the audience can chant along to or accompany with a musical instrument. For example, the elephant's music can be reproduced with a drum, the monkey's with a *shekere*, the crane's with a thumb piano, and the frog's with a wooden frog guiro.

Mouse & Lion, by Rand Burkert and illustrated by Nancy Ekholm Burkert (Scholastic, 2011).

In this retelling of Aesop's fable, a triangle can represent the mouse and a drum can represent the lion.

Enhance Storytelling

Some stories have moments in them when instruments can be used to represent an action or add to the drama of the story:

Jungle Drums, by Graeme Base (Harry N. Abrams, 2004).

Children can pound drums when the main character Ngiri plays his drums.

Shake-It-Up Tales! Stories to Sing, Dance, Drum, and Act Out, by Margaret Read MacDonald (August House, 2000).

This collection has three tales that can be enhanced with drums or shakers. "Fari Mbam," a Wolof folktale from Gambia, is about a donkey king who leaves home. His followers miss him and search for him. Everywhere they stop, they sing and drum a song. In "The Big Man Drum," a Dai folktale from China, Yan relaxes outside with eyes closed. Monkeys discover him and aren't quite sure what he is. Even though the monkeys start drumming on his stomach, Yan doesn't move. When he makes sounds, the monkeys believe that he is a "Big Man Drum." The rest of the story involves jewels and a greedy rich man. My favorite story out of the collection, "Baby Rattlesnake's First Rattle," is a Pawnee tale about a baby snake who really wants a rattle even though he is too young. When he is given the rattle, he plays some jokes on unsuspecting animals. MacDonald suggests shaking a maraca to represent the snake's rattle. I like to hide my maraca and shake it behind my back or under a table when telling the story. The first time I shake the maraca, children are always surprised.

Play Melodies

Instruments can be used to play melodies. Kazoos are fun for this. Pick out short songs with simple melodies, like nursery rhymes, and encourage children to hum along. You can also perform a nursery rhyme or traditional song using a kazoo and see if the children can guess the title.

Children can also play melodies using handbells or boomwhackers (percussion tubes). Each bell or percussion tube represents a note on a scale. Ring the corresponding bell or tap the individual tube to play a note in a song. Once again, you could play the instruments yourself or pass them out to children and direct them to play their note when it's their turn.

Refocus a Group

Percussion and rhythm can be an effective way to refocus a group and gather attention. One of the schools that I visit uses this technique for room management: Whenever a large group gets loud, the teacher claps out a rhythm that the students then imitate. They do this several times to different rhythms until everyone is focused on the teacher. You could tap out a rhythm on a drum or with rhythm sticks during a library program. The key is to teach children the concept at the beginning of the program so that they know what to do when you use it later on.

You can also use a specific instrument to gather attention. Tell children that when they hear the sound of the triangle, kazoo, or xylophone, it's time for them to quiet down for the next activity.

Putting Instruments Away

After instrument time, sing or play a song to help children put their instruments away. Here are some examples:

▶ "Our Instruments," by Cindy Brown

Our instruments are quiet now.
Hold instrument to chest or make a "shhh" motion.
Let's put them on the floor.
Place instrument on floor in front of you.
Our hands are folded in our laps.
Fold hand in laps.
We're listening once more.   *Wiggle ears.*

▶ "Put Your Instruments Away," from the recording *Play Your Instruments and Make a Pretty Sound*, by Ella Jenkins (Smithsonian/Folkways Records, 1994), is a song that you can play to encourage children to put their instruments away.

▶ "Good-bye Instruments," sung to the tune of "London Bridge":

> Now it's time to say good-bye, say good-bye, say good-bye.
> Now it's time to say good-bye to our instruments.
> Now it's time to put them away, put them away, put them away.
> Now it's time to put them away until next time.

CHAPTER 3
INSTRUMENT JAM BAND

nstruments have been around for thousands of years, and they continue to evolve with the use and needs of musicians. In this chapter, we explore the wide variety of instruments and the sounds they make. To prepare for the theme, gather a variety of instruments. These could be band or orchestra instruments, folk instruments, homemade instruments, or a combination of these. If you don't have instruments or have only a small sampling, ask your neighbors and coworkers if they have any that they would be willing to share. Talk to the teens in your library. If you have a community orchestra or band, consider inviting some of the members to the program.

To introduce the theme, hold up instruments like a trumpet or a triangle and ask children to describe what the instrument is made of and what it sounds like. You can also share interesting facts from nonfiction books about instruments.

PROGRAM PLAYLIST

- ▶ Opening Song: "Bagpipes," from the recording *Jim Gill Presents Music Play for Folks of All Stripes*, by Jim Gill
- ▶ Book: *Catfish Kate and the Sweet Swamp Band*, by Sarah Weeks and illustrated by Elwood H. Smith
- ▶ Song: "I Was Born a Horn," from the recording *Jim Gill Presents Music Play for Folks of All Stripes*, by Jim Gill
- ▶ Book: *Song of Middle C*, by Alison McGhee and illustrated by Scott Menchin
- ▶ Song: "Instrument of the Day," from the recording *Everyone Loves to Dance!* by Aaron Nigel Smith

- ▶ Book: *Woof: A Love Story,* by Sarah Weeks and illustrated by Holly Berry
- ▶ Song: "I Was Born to Blow This Horn," by Michael-Leon Wooley, from the recording *Bayou Boogie*
- ▶ Book: *Listen to My Trumpet!* by Mo Willems
- ▶ Activity: Guess the Instrument
- ▶ Musical Instrument: Rain stick

Opening Song

"Bagpipes," from the recording *Jim Gill Presents Music Play for Folks of All Stripes,* by Jim Gill (Jim Gill Music, 2011).
Bagpipes have a very distinctive sound. In this song, they cause Gill (and listeners) to do different physical movements. Each action builds on another, so that at the end of the song listeners are doing all four movements.

Book

Catfish Kate and the Sweet Swamp Band, by Sarah Weeks and illustrated by Elwood H. Smith (Atheneum Books for Young Readers, 2009).
Catfish Kate and her Sweet Swamp Band jam all night long. Skink and his Skunktail Boys want to read in quiet. They go head-to-head, girls versus boys. Will one group win, or can they find a middle ground?

Song

"I Was Born a Horn," from the recording *Jim Gill Presents Music Play for Folks of All Stripes,* by Jim Gill (Jim Gill Music, 2011).
Use this song to introduce the four sections of an orchestra: brass, percussion, strings, and woodwinds. Children can pretend to play the various instruments.

Book

Song of Middle C, by Alison McGhee and illustrated by Scott Menchin (Candlewick Press, 2009).
The young girl in this story practices and practices. To prepare for her piano recital, she even wears her lucky clothes, including her lucky under-

wear. She's ready to play "Dance of the Wood Elves," but then it happens—she forgets her piece. The only thing left to do is improvise.

Song

"Instrument of the Day," from the recording *Everyone Loves to Dance!* **by Aaron Nigel Smith (Music for Little People, 2010).**
    What's the instrument of the day? Have children listen to the sound of each instrument as it is highlighted in the song: horn, drums, piano, guitar, and accordion. Afterward, ask them to name their favorite instrument.

Book

Woof: A Love Story, **by Sarah Weeks and illustrated by Holly Berry (HarperCollins Children's Books, 2009).**
    Dog loves Cat, but when he tries to tell Cat how he feels, all she hears is "woof" and "grrr." Dog eventually gives up and consoles himself with digging in the dirt. That's when he discovers a new kind of bone, a trombone, and uses music to share his feelings with Cat.

Song

"I Was Born to Blow This Horn," by Michael-Leon Wooley, from the recording *Bayou Boogie* **(Walt Disney Records, 2010).**
    A trumpet player shares his musical story and his passion for playing the horn. Children can keep the beat by clapping their hands or snapping their fingers.

Book

Listen to My Trumpet! **by Mo Willems (Hyperion Books for Children, 2012).**
    Piggie is extremely excited to play his trumpet for Elephant. Elephant isn't sure what kind of noise is coming out of Piggie's trumpet, but it definitely isn't music. This is a fun story to tell in tandem with another person. One person can be Elephant and the other Piggie. If you have access to a trumpet, you can "play" the trumpet parts during the story.

Activity
Guess the Instrument

Test children's instrument acumen by having children close their eyes, and then play a musical instrument and see if they can guess what it is. If you don't have musical instruments, use the CD-ROM from *Those Amazing Musical Instruments! Your Guide to the Orchestra through Sounds and Stories,* by Genevieve Helsby (Sourcebooks Jabberwocky, 2007), which has short sound clips for instruments.

Musical Instrument
Rain Stick

Supplies:
- ▶ Paper-towel tube, 1 for each child
- ▶ Construction paper, cut into 4-inch-by-4-inch squares, 2 pieces for each child
- ▶ Heavy-duty aluminum foil, 5 inches by 18 inches, 1 for each child
- ▶ Rice
- ▶ Masking or duct tape
- ▶ Decorating supplies

Directions:
- ▶ Decorate the paper-towel tube with markers or stickers.
- ▶ Attach a construction-paper square to one end of the tube with tape.
- ▶ Slightly crumple and twist one strip of foil.
- ▶ Place foil in the tube so that it extends from the top to the bottom of the tube.
- ▶ Add a handful of rice.
- ▶ Attach a construction-paper square to the open end of the tube.
- ▶ Flip the finished rain stick from top to bottom. As the rice hits the foil, it will sound like rain.

BONUS BOOKS

Acoustic Rooster and His Barnyard Band, by Kwame Alexander and illustrated by Tim Bowers (Sleeping Bear Press, 2011).

It's the Barnyard Talent Show and Acoustic Rooster needs a band. He tries out a variety of groups—Thelonious Monkey's crew, Mules Davis's orchestra, Ella Finchgerald's trio—but he doesn't fit in with any of them. He decides that the best option is to create his own ensemble. Use this story to introduce children to the jazz greats. Included is a jazz time line and glossary with music vocabulary and facts about famous musicians and songs.

Clink, by Kelly DiPucchio and illustrated by Matthew Myers (Balzer + Bray, 2011).

Robot Clink used to make perfect toast and music. Over the years, he begins to rust and fall apart. All he does now is hang out at the Robot Shoppe, because no one wants an old robot who burns toast. When a young boy comes in playing music on a harmonica, Clink thinks he may have found a kindred spirit. He perks up, plays a song, and even does a dance. Can the boy look past Clink's rust and loose sprockets to see his potential?

Farmer Joe and the Music Show, by Tony Mitton and illustrated by Guy Parker-Rees (Orchard Books, 2009).

All the animals on the farm have the blues. Farmer Joe has to do something to help his animals, but he isn't sure what. Suddenly he has an idea! He grabs his guitar and starts playing some music. Sure enough, the hens perk up enough to peck and lay eggs. Farmer's friend Fox joins in the music making, and suddenly the pigs are eating again. Rabbit doesn't want to be left out, so she adds her concertina to the musical mix. Even the crop of sunflowers begins growing again. The farm is alive with music, dancing, and smiles all around.

Little Pig Joins the Band, by David Hyde Costello (Charlesbridge, 2011).

Grandpa shares his instruments with Little Pig and his brothers and sisters. Each sibling chooses the perfect instrument, but Little Pig, who is too little to play the drum, trombone, trumpet, and tuba, has a hard time finding his place in the band. As Little Pig laments that he's too little for the band, he finds a perfect role—as leader.

Peter and the Wolf, by Chris Raschka (Atheneum Books for Young Readers, 2008).

Raschka has several musical picture books. In this one, he creates a stage version of Sergei Prokofiev's *Peter and the Wolf* composition. In Prokofiev's piece, an instrument represents each character in the story. Although no music accompanies the picture book, you can introduce the story to children and ask them to think about what instruments each animal can be represented with. After the conclusion, which has a surprise ending different from the original version, encourage children to share which instrument they associated with each animal. You may even want to play clips from Prokofiev's work.

BONUS TRACKS

"Be Part of the Band," from the recording *A Family Album,* **by the Verve Pipe (LMNO Pop, 2009).**

It's fun to be in a band. All you need to do is start playing an instrument.

Jim Gill's Irrational Anthem and More Salutes to Nonsense, **by Jim Gill (Jim Gill Music, 2001).**

In "Follow the Band," children can pretend that they are part of the band and clap along to each instrument's rhythm. In "Saxophones," children hear the different types of saxophones: baritone, tenor sax, alto sax, and soprano.

"Mr. Bassman (and Piano Girl)," from the recording *Rocketship Run,* **by the Laurie Berkner Band (Two Tomatoes Records, 2008).**

Mr. Bassman and Piano Girl have their own special music. Mr. Bassman sounds deep and low. Piano Girl tickles across the keys drawing out a range of notes light and lively.

Play Your Instruments and Make a Pretty Sound, **by Ella Jenkins (Smithsonian/ Folkways Records, 1994).**

Use the recording to introduce instrument play to a group. *Play Your Instruments and Make a Pretty Sound* helps children understand the idea of music versus noise. Jenkins demonstrates a lot of different rhythm instruments. If you don't have those instruments but are comfortable with the tune, you can sing the song without the CD and mention instruments that you do have. "Put Your Instruments Away" creates an orderly process for returning instruments to their home.

"Tromboning," from the recording *Jim Gill Sings Moving Rhymes for Modern Times,* **by Jim Gill (Jim Gill Music, 2005).**

Gill descriptively paints a picture of a trombonist and how he uses the trombone to bring forth unique and varied sounds.

CHAPTER 4
FEEL THE RHYTHM

ercussion instruments can be hit, shaken, scraped, and tapped. They can be fancy and expensive or created from found objects. Anything can be a percussion instrument. Some musicians use their body as a percussion instrument and tap their hands on their chest or their knees to create music.

One way to start the program is to ask children to name percussion instruments. What makes them percussion instead of string or woodwind instruments? Then hold up some items from home: a trash bin, a paper plate, a large spoon, and a whisk, and ask them whether they think these are percussion instruments. Invite children to come up and show how each item can be transformed into a percussion instrument. For example, tapping a wooden spoon on a trash can or tapping two paper plates together makes them percussion instruments.

PROGRAM PLAYLIST

- ▶ Opening Song: "Willie and the Hand Jive," by Taj Mahal and Linda Tillery, from the recording *Rock & Roll Playground*
- ▶ Book: *Tortuga in Trouble*, by Ann Whitford Paul and illustrated by Ethan Long
- ▶ Song: "Jim Along Josie," from the recording *Ladybug Music: Pink Collection*, by Ladybug Music
- ▶ Book: *Be Quiet, Mike!* by Leslie Patricelli

- ▶ Song: "Pots and Pans," by the Bacon Brothers, from the songbook and CD *Dog Train: Deluxe Illustrated Lyrics Book of the Unpredictable Rock-and-Roll Journey*, by Sandra Boynton
- ▶ Book: *Teach Your Buffalo to Play Drums*, by Audrey Vernick and illustrated by Daniel Jennewein
- ▶ Song: "Mary Mack," by Ella Jenkins, from the recording *Smithsonian Folkways Children's Music Collection*
- ▶ Book: *Jungle Drums*, by Graeme Base
- ▶ Activity: Rhythm Mirror
- ▶ Musical Instrument: Drum

Opening Song

"Willie and the Hand Jive," by Taj Mahal and Linda Tillery, from the recording *Rock & Roll Playground* (Putumayo World Music, 2010).
Pass out shakers, and children can play along with the rhythm of the song, or you can teach children to do the hand jive. The hand jive is a series of movements, each one repeated twice. You can see it used in the movie *Grease.* You can also find examples of people doing the hand jive on YouTube. To help children learn the motions, you can slow down the tempo and have children repeat each action four times instead of two.

Book

Tortuga in Trouble, by Ann Whitford Paul and illustrated by Ethan Long (Holiday House, 2009).
Tortuga, a tortoise, is on his way to Grandmother's house with a basketful of yummy treats: *ensalada*, tamales, and flan. His friends Iguana, the rabbit Conejo, and the snake Culebra want to travel with Tortuga to "help," but mostly to eat the yummy food. Even though Tortuga doesn't need their help, the friends continue to secretly trail after him. Like Little Red Riding Hood, when Tortuga makes it to Grandmother's house, she doesn't quite look as he remembers. Coyote has heard about the delicious food and has his own devious plan. Tortuga's friends create a racket using their tails and feet to frighten Coyote and save Tortuga and the *ensalada*, tamales, and flan. To make the story interactive, provide three types of instruments for children so that when they get to the point at which Iguana,

Conejo, and Culebra make noise, they can join in. For Iguana, try clappers or rhythm sticks; for Culebra, shakers; and for Conejo, drums.

Song

"Jim Along Josie," from the recording *Ladybug Music: Pink Collection*, by Ladybug Music (Ladybug Music, 2011).

This version of a traditional song has great percussion. Have children listen to the music and guess what the instruments might be. The percussion is complicated and fast, so replicating the exact rhythm will be difficult. Instead, have children clap or tap two pencils or rhythm sticks together in a steady rhythm as they listen to the song.

Book

Be Quiet, Mike! by Leslie Patricelli (Candlewick Press, 2011).

Feeling the beat in his body, Mike can't but help express it by making everything into percussion instruments. He turns tennis rackets and trash cans into drums and uses his silverware to tap out a rhythm on the dining room table. Not everyone likes his music, though. In fact, family and neighbors alike are always telling him to quiet down. Nevertheless, Mike can't stop. One day he falls in love with a drum set, one that he can't afford. Mike doesn't let that get him down. He has a plan. The endpapers show a variety of percussion instruments, including some household objects that Mike uses to create music.

Song

"Pots and Pans," by the Bacon Brothers, from the songbook and CD *Dog Train: Deluxe Illustrated Lyrics Book of the Unpredictable Rock-And-Roll Journey* by Sandra Boynton (Workman Publishing, 2005).

The Bacon Brothers play music using objects from the kitchen. Children can keep the beat with rhythm sticks or with kitchen instruments like a wooden spoon and the lid from a pot.

Book

Teach Your Buffalo to Play Drums, by Audrey Vernick and illustrated by Daniel Jennewein (Balzer + Bray, 2011).

Imagine you own a pet buffalo. Maybe not the best idea, but in time everyone becomes fond of him. Buffalo wants to play drums, and it's your job to show him what to do. At first you're skeptical about his interest because Buffalo has a short attention span. He likes to learn how to do all kinds of things including ice-skating and surfing. Then he moves on to something else, and those items end up in a closet. You determine to teach him anyway. What does it take to be a drummer? Can a big creature like Buffalo play the drums successfully? Share this humorous story to answer those questions.

Song

"Mary Mack," by Ella Jenkins, from the recording *Smithsonian Folkways Children's Music Collection* (Smithsonian Folkways Recordings, 1998).
Teach children how to do different clapping patterns to this song. For instance, children can do a pattern of clapping their hands and tapping the floor (clap, tap, clap, tap), or they can pair up and learn a hand-clapping game. Directions for one version of a game can be found in the book *Miss Mary Mack*, by Mary Ann Hoberman and illustrated by Nadine Bernard Westcott (Little, Brown, and Company, 1998). You can also find a version on DLTK's website (www.dltk-kids.com/games/miss_mary_mack_clapping_game.htm).

Book

Jungle Drums, by Graeme Base (Harry N. Abrams, 2004).
Ngiri Mdogo, a small, unassuming warthog, wishes that he could be handsome like the other dashing rain-forest animals, with their colorful spots, stripes, and unique features. Old Nyumbu hears his wish and gives him bongos and instructions to beat the drums when making a wish. He cautions Ngiri to be careful, because sometimes wishes don't exactly work out as planned. That night Ngiri plays the drums and makes another wish. The next day Ngiri hasn't changed, but the rest of the warthogs have spots and color and distinctive beautiful traits. The warthogs relish in their new beauty. The rest of the animals are angry because they are now plain. When it is nighttime, Ngiri plays his drums. Once again, his wish doesn't work exactly as he wants. Will Ngiri be able to fix the mess he has created? Have children tap out a rhythm on homemade drums when Ngiri plays the drums at night. It can be a simple rhythm—like tap, tap, boom—with children tapping the top of the drum twice and then slapping the side of the drum on the "boom" or a more complex rhythm. If you don't have drums, children can use their body as drums and tap out rhythms on the tops of their thighs and arms or hands.

Activity
Rhythm Mirror

Clap a rhythm and have children repeat it. Start with slow and short rhythms. Once children get the hang of those, try rhythms that include clapping and tapping a body part like knees or chest. Once children are comfortable with the new rhythms, pass out an instrument and have children mirror patterns using the instruments.

Musical Instrument
Drum

Supplies:
- ▶ Cylindrical containers, such as coffee cans, potato-chip or oatmeal containers, aluminum cans: 1 container per child
- ▶ Decorating materials
- ▶ Contact paper to make lids
- ▶ Masking tape or duct tape to securely attach the lid to the container

Directions:
- ▶ Decorate the outside of the cylindrical container.
- ▶ If the container has a lid and you like the sound the drum makes when you tap the lid, tape the lid to the container, and the drum is done.
- ▶ If it doesn't have a lid or if you don't like the lid, attach a piece of contact paper to the container to make a lid.
- ▶ Once children have decorated their drums, play some music, like the song "Mary Mack," so they can drum along.

BONUS BOOKS

Around the World with the Percussion Family! **by Trisha Speed Shaskan and illustrated by Robert Meganck (Picture Window Books, 2011).**
Instruments like the xylophone, the tambourine, the bass drum, and cymbals make up the percussion family. Travel the globe and discover interesting facts about percussion instruments and their history.

Drum City, **by Thea Guidone and illustrated by Vanessa Newton (Tricycle Press, 2010).**

Grab your pots, your whisks, your sticks, and your trash-can lids, and join the drum parade! After reading the book, give children the chance to use household items to make their own drum sounds. Create a parade line and march around the room to the rhythm. Milkshake has a marching song titled "Parade," on the recording *Play!* (Milkshake Music, 2007), which goes along well with this book.

Drums, **by Cynthia Amoroso and Robert B. Noyed (Child's World, 2010).**

Part of the Music Makers series, *Drums* has basic introductory information about drums for beginning readers. It includes information about what drums look like, what people used them for in the past, and how we use them now.

Drums and Percussion Instruments, **by Anita Ganeri (Smart Apple Media, 2012).**

Explore the many types of percussion instruments, from kettledrums to castanets and from steel drums to gongs. Illustrations highlight the various parts of percussion instruments, and photos show them in use. Pick a few facts to share with your audience.

Little Man, **by Dionne Warwick and David Freeman Wooley and illustrated by Fred Willingham (Charlesbridge, 2011).**

Little Man has a passion for playing the drums. When he notices a bike for sale, he falls in love with the bike and the opportunity it would provide him to take music lessons. Coming up with the money for a bike takes time and hard work, just like playing the drums. Will Little Man ever be able to buy the bike and play the drums like he wants? The story, based on David Freeman Wooley's life, also includes a CD with a track of Dionne Warwick reading the story and a track with Wooley talking about and playing the different drums in a drum set.

Lola's Fandango, **by Anna Witte and illustrated by Micha Archer (Barefoot Books, 2011).**

One day Lola discovers her mother's flamenco shoes. Her mother doesn't want to talk about them, so Lola approaches her father. He tells her that her mother used to be a dancer. Lola asks her father to secretly teach her the flamenco. Later, her father wants her to dance for her mother's birthday, but Lola is nervous. Included is a CD with the Amador family (Rosi and Brian, members of the Latin band Sol y Canto, and their two daughters) reading the story and performing flamenco music.

Knick Knack Paddy Whack, **by SteveSongs and illustrated by Christiane Engel (Barefoot Books, 2008).**

> In the counting song, "This Old Man" plays the drum for one child. Each verse introduces a new child and a new instrument. SteveSongs performs the song on the accompanying CD. At the beginning of each verse, the new instrument has a short solo. Have children listen to the song and guess what the instrument is. If they aren't sure, they can look at the illustrations for another clue. The CD also has a musical track without the lyrics. A score with chords is included at the end of the book, along with a page of information about instrument families.

¡Olé! Flamenco, **by George Ancona (Lee & Low Books, 2010).**

> Ancona uses photos and facts to help children visualize the movement and energy of flamenco dancing. Originating from Spain, the music and dance have evolved over time and can now be found around the world. Flamenco dancers establish rhythm in several ways, through hand clapping, finger snapping, using castanets, or tapping the floor in certain ways with their shoes.

The Steel Pan Man of Harlem, **by Colin Bootman (Carolrhoda Books, 2009).**

> The streets of Harlem are overridden with rats in this story. A stranger who plays the steel pan comes to town and performs the most enthralling music. Everyone is spellbound, even the rats. The Steel Pan Man tells the mayor that he can take care of the rats for a price, one million dollars. Can the Steel Pan Man save the city? And will he get his million dollars? This updated version of Robert Browning's poem "The Pied Piper of Hamelin" takes place during the Harlem Renaissance.

BONUS TRACKS

Banjo to Beatbox, **by Cathy and Marcy, with Christylez Bacon (Community Music, 2009).**

> "It's the Beat Box" illustrates how you can make a plethora of percussion sounds using your mouth and voice. How do you play a washboard? Listen and play along to "Syncopated Washboard Rhythm Song."

"Campo," from the recording *Hot Peas 'n Butter,* **vol. 2,** *A Second Helping,* **by Hot Peas 'n Butter (Hot Peas 'n Butter, 2010).**

> This bilingual English and Spanish song introduces percussion instruments like the conga, the guiro, and the shaker.

"Drumming the House," from the recording *Jim Gill Sings Moving Rhymes for Modern Times*, **by Jim Gill (Jim Gill Music, 2005).**

Listen to the different sounds of the drum set and then hear what it sounds like to drum on various parts of the house, like the sink, the table, and the stairs.

"The Gong Song," from the recording *Jim Gill's Irrational Anthem and More Salutes to Nonsense*, **by Jim Gill (Jim Gill Music, 2001).**

This is a short, silly nonsense song about Kevin and his gong.

"Mama Don't Allow No Jugband Music 'Round Here," from the recording *Maria Muldaur's Barnyard Dance: Jug Band Music for Kids*, **by Maria Muldaur (Music for Little People, 2010).**

Muldaur uses all kinds of interesting percussion instruments, including a washboard and a desk bell in her jug-band music. You can purchase a washboard for less than twenty dollars. They are fun to play, and they make different sounds depending on what you use to run up and down the ridges. Some people put thimbles on their fingers to play the washboard. Another version of the song "Mama Don't Allow" can be found on *Sing along with Sam* (Hullabaloo, 2006). Mama doesn't allow music to be played, including clapping, stomping, or finger snapping.

"More Cowbell," from the recording *I'm a Rock Star*, **by Joanie Leeds and the Nightlights (Limbostar, 2010).**

Everything is better with a little bit more cowbell. Shakers, the tambourine, and the triangle are in the song as well.

CHAPTER 5
SING-ALONG STORIES AND SONGS

e sing all the time. We sing in the shower, in the car, and in group settings like birthday parties and sporting events. If you ask people if they can sing, though, frequently you'll get the response, "Oh, no! I'm not any good." Children don't care about that. A good voice or perfect pitch doesn't matter. Children like to sing, and they like to sing with you.

Ask children about their favorite song, singer, and band. Are there particular times when they like to sing? Tell them that they are going to sing a lot during the next hour, so they need to warm up their vocal chords with a special song.

PROGRAM PLAYLIST

- ▶ Opening Song: "Ola with Didjuridu Train Ride," from the recording *Rhythm Train*, by Leslie Bixler and Chad Smith, and featuring Dick Van Dyke
- ▶ Book: *ZooZical*, by Judy Sierra and illustrated by Marc Brown
- ▶ Song: "Boom Chicka Boom," from the recording *Let's Go! Travel, Camp and Car Songs*, by Susie Tallman and Friends
- ▶ Book: *Abiyoyo Returns*, by Pete Seeger and Paul DuBois Jacobs and illustrated by Michael Hays
- ▶ Song: "Chewing Gum," from the book and CD *Lisa Loeb's Silly Sing-Along: The Disappointing Pancake and Other Zany Songs*, by Lisa Loeb and illustrated by Ryan O'Rourke

- ▶ Book: *When Louis Armstrong Taught Me Scat*, by Muriel Harris Weinstein and illustrated by R. Gregory Christie
- ▶ Song: "Scat Like That," from the recording *Scat Like That: A Musical Word Odyssey*, by Cathy Fink and Marcy Marxer
- ▶ Book: *Pete the Cat: I Love My White Shoes*, by Eric Litwin and illustrated by James Dean
- ▶ Activity: "The Telephone Game," from *Lisa Loeb's Silly Sing-Along: The Disappointing Pancake and Other Zany Songs*, by Lisa Loeb and illustrated by Ryan O'Rourke
- ▶ Musical Instrument: Tambourine

Opening Song

"Ola with Didjuridu Train Ride," from the recording *Rhythm Train*, by Leslie Bixler and Chad Smith, and featuring Dick Van Dyke (Leslie Bixler, 2009).
The song is kind of like a vocal exercise. It begins with children saying hello in different languages. Next they sing high and low, then make sounds like a fire-truck siren, a ghost, a cat, a witch, and more. The end of the track has a conversation that leads into the next song on the CD. If you don't want to use the second song in your program, stop the track as soon as the singing is done.

Book

***ZooZical*, by Judy Sierra and illustrated by Marc Brown (Alfred A. Knopf, 2011).**
It's winter and the zoo animals are bored, with nothing to do and few people visiting. They have the winter blues until two baby animals, a hippo and a kangaroo, come up with the exciting idea to put on a "ZooZical," a mixture of song and dance. The zoo animals take a variety of children's songs and adapt them. For example, they perform lines from "For He's a Jolly Gorilla," "Oh My Darling Porcupine," and "Zoo Hokey Pokey."

Song

"Boom Chicka Boom," from the recording *Let's Go! Travel, Camp and Car Songs*, by Susie Tallman and Friends (Rock Me Baby Records, 2007).
This echo song is sung multiple times, but each time in a different voice.

For example, one time it is sung as Elvis would sing it. Another time it sounds like an opera singer is performing it. Encourage children to sing the song using those different voices.

Book

Abiyoyo Returns, by Pete Seeger and Paul DuBois Jacobs and illustrated by Michael Hays (Aladdin, 2004).

In the sequel to *Abiyoyo* (Simon and Schuster, 2001), townsfolk discover the importance of sharing food and songs. To remove an enormous boulder, the townspeople decide to use Grandpa's magic to raise the giant Abiyoyo. They develop a plan to use Abiyoyo's strength and then send him away with magic, but their plan has a hiccup. "Abiyoyo" is one of my favorite songs to teach kids. The musical score is included at the end of the story, but if you aren't sure about the tune, Pete Seeger performs the song on *Abiyoyo and Other Story Songs for Children* (Smithsonian Folkways, 1992). Once I teach children the song, we practice singing it slow, medium, and then super fast. We also practice it softly and then very loudly. This is a song that children love singing with gusto.

Song

"Chewing Gum," from the book and CD *Lisa Loeb's Silly Sing-Along: The Disappointing Pancake and Other Zany Songs*, by Lisa Loeb and illustrated by Ryan O'Rourke (Sterling Children's Books, 2011).

The book contains a selection of silly songs, illustrations, and activities. It also has a CD of Loeb performing the songs. "Chewing Gum" has an easy chorus for children to learn.

Book

When Louis Armstrong Taught Me Scat, by Muriel Harris Weinstein and illustrated by R. Gregory Christie (Chronicle Books, 2008).

Introduce children to a type of improvisational singing known as scat. A young girl learns about scat singing from her mother. That night in a dream Louis Armstrong visits her and gifts her with a singing lesson. Together they scat about bubble gum. The author has included biographical information about Louis Armstrong and a short history of scat. Follow the story with a chance for children to do their own scat singing.

Song

"Scat Like That," from the recording *Scat Like That: A Musical Word Odyssey*, by Cathy Fink and Marcy Marxer (Rounder Records, 2005).
Embrace the use of syllables and sounds and learn to scat with an upbeat song. Parts of the song are echoed. The scat sections start easier at first and then become a bit longer and more complex. Another one that teaches children how to scat is "Scat Like That," from *On the Move*, by Greg and Steve (Youngheart Records, 1983).

Book

***Pete the Cat: I Love My White Shoes*, by Eric Litwin and illustrated by James Dean (HarperCollins, 2010).**
Nothing fazes Pete the Cat. Although he loves his white shoes and has a special song for them, he doesn't get upset when he steps in blueberries and his shoes turn blue or when he steps in mud and they become brown. If you like the story, be sure to check out the sequel, *Pete the Cat: Rocking in My School Shoes* (HarperCollins, 2011). Pete reads, eats, plays, and more in his favorite school shoes. The repetition in the songs "Rocking in My School Shoes" and "I Love My White Shoes" makes these easy and fun for children to sing and finger snap along to. (Visit www.ericlitwin.com or www .harpercollinschildrens.com/feature/petethecat to hear Pete's songs).

Activity

"The Telephone Game," from *Lisa Loeb's Silly Sing-Along: The Disappointing Pancake and Other Zany Songs*, by Lisa Loeb and illustrated by Ryan O'Rourke (Sterling Children's Books, 2011).
It's the old game of telephone. Have one child quietly share a sentence with another who will then share the same sentence with another child. Slowly the sentence will work its way from child to child until it comes full circle to the person who began the game. Then it's time to see how close the original statement is to the ending statement.

Musical Instrument
Tambourine

Supplies:
- ▶ Paper plates: 1 per child
- ▶ Jingle bells: 4 per child
- ▶ Yarn: 1 piece of yarn per child (the yarn should be long enough to go around the circumference of the paper plate)
- ▶ Tape
- ▶ Hole punch
- ▶ Decorating materials

Directions:
- ▶ Before the program, punch four holes around the edge of the plates.
- ▶ Cut pieces of yarn long enough to circle the paper plate.
- ▶ Attach tape to one end of each piece of yarn to make the yarn similar to a shoelace, so it will be easier for children to thread the yarn through the holes of the plate and the jingle bells.
- ▶ Have children decorate the paper plate.
- ▶ After decorating, have children thread the yarn through one of the holes in the paper plate and attach a jingle bell. They should repeat this with the other holes in the plate. Then tie the two ends of yarn together in a knot.
- ▶ When children shake the paper plate or hit it on their hand or thigh, the bells will jingle. Play "I Love My White Shoes" or "Boom Chicka Boom" again and have children play their tambourines.

BONUS BOOKS

All God's Critters, by Bill Staines and illustrated by Kadir Nelson (Simon and Schuster Books for Young Readers, 2009).
The song by Bill Staines and illustrations by Kadir Nelson emphasize the theme that everyone can sing. Every animal (ox, fox, hippo, donkey, and more) and every type of singing voice (loud, soft, howling, mooing) has a place in the choir. Nelson's lovely illustrations feature a variety of animals belting out a joyous song. Included at the end of the picture book is a musical score.

Ant and Grasshopper, **by Luli Gray and illustrated by Giuliano Ferri (Margaret K. McElderry, 2011).**

Ant works diligently and loves to count all of the food that he has accumulated throughout the summer and fall season. At the same time Grasshopper spends his days singing and playing his fiddle, much to Ant's dismay. When winter sets in, Grasshopper asks for food from Ant, but Ant sends him away. Afterward, Ant has problems counting and finds himself dreaming about music. Will Ant and Grasshopper learn to help each other? The story ends with both Ant and Grasshopper singing a funny song, "Here We Come a Waffle-ing," which you can teach to participants.

Chirchir Is Singing, **by Kelly Cunnane and illustrated by Jude Daly (Schwartz & Wade Books, 2011).**

In a village in Africa a young girl named Chirchir tries to help her family members with chores like gathering water from the well and digging potatoes, but her clumsiness causes more problems than help. Chirchir sings a song for every chore she tries. After struggling to help with many chores and not having positive experiences, she recognizes that her talent for singing can help her finally complete one very special chore. Create your own tune to sing Chirchir's songs to or try adapting them to traditional tunes like "Twinkle, Twinkle, Little Star."

Floating on Mama's Song / Flotando en la canción de mamá, **by Laura Lacámara and illustrated by Yuyi Morales (Katherine Tegen Books, 2010).**

Share this bilingual English-Spanish story to talk about the magic of singing. Anita loves her mama's singing, but something crazy happens when her mama sings. It's so infectious that anyone who hears her voice floats in the air, including the neighborhood animals. When Grandma finds out, she tells Mama it's too dangerous for her to sing. Mama promises that she will stop. Sadness envelops her, the neighborhood, and the animals. Anita uncovers a family secret that helps her mother rediscover the gift of song.

Little Diva, **by LaChanze and illustrated by Brian Pinkney (Feiwel and Friends, 2010).**

Nena is a DIT, a diva in training. She does vocal exercises, practices bowing, and experiments with hair and makeup—all part of the very serious training to be like her mother, a real diva and Broadway star. Nena is an energetic, enthusiastic child who shares her excitement for singing, dancing, and performing just like her mom. An accompanying CD features LaChanze singing a song about diva training.

Paula Bunyan, **by Phyllis Root and illustrated by Kevin O'Malley (Farrar, Straus, and Giroux, 2009).**

Ever hear of Paula Bunyan, sister to Paul? Paula likes to sing, but people get really cranky when they hear her music because her voice ruptures glass. Paula takes her tunes north to an isolated area where she can sing whenever she wants and not bother humans. She has adventures like teaching wolves to sing "Row, Row, Row Your Boat" and making friends with a bear. One day she sees a field of trees demolished by lumberjacks. Paula wants to save the land, but has she finally met her match?

Pepi Sings a New Song, **by Laura Ljungkvist (Beach Lane Books, 2010).**

Pepi the parrot loves to sing, and his owner, Peter, loves outer space. Pepi sings the same song about space every night. Over time he can tell that Peter is bored. Pepi sets out to find new inspiration for his music. He visits the bakery, a music studio, an art studio, a market, and a dog park, where he learns all kinds of words to use in his music. He incorporates this insight to create a song for Peter. Pepi's song about space and his new song are sung to the tune of "Twinkle, Twinkle, Little Star." After reading the book, brainstorm additional words that can be used in Pepi's song. Create another song using those words. For example:

Twinkle, twinkle lots of books
Facts about pets and recipes for cooks
Adventure, fantasy, science fiction, poetry
Funny, scary, historical, mystery
Making robots, drawing cats
Learning about balls and baseball bats.

Small Florence: Piggy Pop Star! **by Claire Alexander (Albert Whitman, 2010).**

Florence's size causes her older sisters to underestimate her and her singing ability, but that doesn't prevent Florence from practicing secretly by herself and cautiously with her barnyard friends. When a singing competition comes to town, Florence asks if she can perform with her sisters, but they tell her no. On the big day, the sisters experience stage fright, and a little pig named Florence saves the day.

The Talent Show, **by Jo Hodgkinson (Anderson Press USA, 2011).**

Bear, Lion, Snake, and Croc form a band for a talent show, but they are missing something very important—a lead singer. A bird volunteers, but the band members say that he is too small. Bird comes up with a plan to prove he should be the band's new singer.

Thelonious Mouse, **by Orel Protopopescu and illustrated by Anne Wilsdorf (Farrar, Straus, and Giroux, 2011).**

Thelonious Mouse is so consumed with music, rhythm, and improvisation that he forgets about his personal safety. He has to finish his songs even if it means he might do something to wake up Fat Cat. His family doesn't understand his musical compulsion, but maybe, just maybe, Fat Cat does.

BONUS TUNES

cELLAbration! A Tribute to Ella Jenkins **(Smithsonian Folkways Recordings, 2004).**

On this CD, different artists perform some of Ella Jenkins's more popular songs. "You'll Sing a Song and I'll Sing a Song," by Cathy Fink, has repetitive phrases that children can sing. This is a good song to use as an introduction to the theme if you are doing the program in the winter, since the lyrics mention singing in the winter. Everyone likes yodeling, and the song "Let's All Sing a Yodeling Song," by Riders in the Sky, teaches kids how to yodel from a slow, short example to increasingly more complicated patterns. Sweet Honey in the Rock performs "Go Miss Mary Mack," using a unique arrangement. Children can join in with the repetitive phrases and sounds.

"Me Mother Caught a Flea," from the recording *There's a Train . . .,* **by We Kids Rock! (We Kids Rock, 2009).**

This short song is repeated several times with only one word changing, the name of the person featured in the song. Once children know how to sing the song, change the version to mention the names of everyone in your group. Incorporating clapping, snapping, or some kind of additional rhythm instrument would add to the fun.

"Sing a Little Song," from the recording *Sing a Little Song,* **by Brian Vogan and His Good Buddies (Brian Vogan, 2010).**

Even on a dreary day, music can make a bad day good. Join in, sing, and see how a song makes everything better.

"Sing Away the Blues," by Anika Noni Rose, from the recording *Bayou Boogie* **(Walt Disney Records, 2010).**

If you're experiencing the blues, the best thing to do is sing. This song is a great way to start.

"Song in My Tummy," from the recording *The Best of the Laurie Berkner Band*, by the Laurie Berkner Band (Two Tomatoes Records, 2010).
Ever hear a song that fills you up and makes you so excited you just have to share? Laurie Berkner has a song that makes its way through different body parts, like the stomach, toes, and nose, and she has to let it free.

CHAPTER 6
MOVING AND GROOVING

 t's hard to listen to music without swaying to the beat, nodding your head, or clapping along to the rhythm. Music and dance are like peanut butter and jelly. Apart they are great, but when you combine the ingredients, they are even better. There are many unique dances in the world and many different dance books. You can do a whole program around ballet, but, as you'll see in this chapter, there are a variety of books that feature other dances.

As an icebreaker, ask children what their favorite type of dance is. Talk about the types of dance they may know, such as hip-hop, line dancing, ballet, tap dancing, and hula dancing. You can also talk about various folk dances, such as the Italian tarantella and the Greek "zorba dance." Music and directions for folk dances can be found on the recording *Folk Dance Fun*, by Georgiana Liccione Stewart (Kimbo, 1984).

PROGRAM PLAYLIST

- ▶ Opening Song: "Ants in Your Pants #99," from the recording *What a Ride!* by Eric Herman and the Invisible Band
- ▶ Book: *Boogie Knights*, by Lisa Wheeler and illustrated by Mark Siegel
- ▶ Song: "The High-Low," from the recording *Radio Wayne*, by Wayne Brady
- ▶ Book: *Fritz Danced the Fandango*, by Alicia Potter and illustrated by Ethan Long

- ▶ Song: "Scootin' Dance Boogie," from the recording *Kid's Country Song and Dance: Action, Sing-Along, Hoe-Down Fun!* by the Learning Station
- ▶ Book: *Brontorina*, by James Howe and illustrated by Randy Cecil
- ▶ Song: "I Changed My Mind," from the recording *Jim Gill Presents Music Play for Folks of All Stripes*, by Jim Gill
- ▶ Book: *Bugtown Boogie*, by Warren Hanson and illustrated by Steve Johnson and Lou Fancher
- ▶ Activity: Ribbon Circles
- ▶ Musical Instrument: Castanets

Opening Song

"Ants in Your Pants #99," from the recording *What a Ride!* by Eric Herman and the Invisible Band (Butter-Dog Records, 2009).
How would you dance if you had ants in your pants? Encourage children to use their imagination and play around with dance moves that match what the band is describing.

Book

***Boogie Knights*, by Lisa Wheeler and illustrated by Mark Siegel (Atheneum Books for Young Readers, 2008).**
It's the middle of the night and the castle is rocking with the Madcap Monster Ball. Werewolves, zombies, mummies, serpents, wizards, and other magical creatures are waltzing, wiggling, sambaing, and even joining a conga line. The seven knights of the castle sleep, oblivious to the dancing mayhem, until each knight is awakened by the ruckus and joins in the dancing. This rhyming story is a great one to start the program, because it features a variety of dances in a funny, entertaining way.

Song

"The High-Low," from the recording *Radio Wayne*, by Wayne Brady (Walt Disney Records, 2011).
Follow Brady's directions and learn a new high-energy dance that incorporates different styles of clapping.

Book

Fritz Danced the Fandango, by Alicia Potter and illustrated by Ethan Long (Scholastic Press, 2009).

Fritz loves to dance the fandango, but the other mountain goats make fun of his hobby. Fritz decides to search for a new herd, a dancing herd. While on the hunt, he meets Liesl, a sheep who likes to yodel, and Gerhard, a dog who plays the glockenspiel. Both mention that they don't fit in either because others don't appreciate their music. Although Fritz finds new friends, he hasn't found a herd that likes to dance. Will Fritz ever find dance partners? The book references words that children might not know: *fandango*, *glockenspiel*, and *yodeling*. The fandango is a Spanish folk dance. The glockenspiel resembles a xylophone but is made of metal instead of wood. Singers who yodel move back and forth between a normal chest voice and a higher falsetto voice.

Song

"Scootin' Dance Boogie," from the recording Kid's Country Song and Dance: Action, Sing-Along, Hoe-Down Fun! by the Learning Station (Monopoli and the Learning Station, 2009).

For those who aren't familiar with country line dancing, this song is a nice introduction, and it's not too fast. Another good line dance is "Pata Pata," an African dance from the recording *Children of the World: Multicultural Rhythmic Activities* (Kimbo Educational, 1991).

Book

Brontorina, by James Howe and illustrated by Randy Cecil (Candlewick Press, 2010).

Brontorina, a dinosaur, has big dreams of dancing ballet, but her size is an issue. She's so large that she hits her head on the ceiling of the dance studio and has to be careful not to crush the other dancers. On top of that, her feet are so big that she doesn't have the right dance shoes. It begins to look like Brontorina is too big to be a dancer—that is, until the dance teacher Madame Lucille comes up with a unique solution. The illustrations are quite funny because Brontorina's size is markedly larger than the students and teacher. Her love of dance and earnestness to learn everything about ballet are endearing.

Song

"I Changed My Mind," from the recording *Jim Gill Presents Music Play for Folks of All Stripes*, **by Jim Gill (Jim Gill Music, 2011).**
Sometimes it's good to dance slowly, and sometimes it's time to dance fast. Children can alternate between making up movements for slow dancing and crazy, fast dancing. You can also have them use ribbon circles or scarves while dancing.

Book

Bugtown Boogie, **by Warren Hanson and illustrated by Steve Johnson and Lou Fancher (HarperCollins Children's Books, 2008).**
A boy walking through the woods at night notices a secret door leading to Bugtown, where many kinds of bugs dance to "a buggie-wuggie beat." Ants, lightning bugs, bees, grasshoppers, centipedes, ladybugs, and more boogie throughout the night. Children who love bugs will enjoy this story and will like looking at the details of the different insects dancing.

Activity
Ribbon Circles

Take objects like shower-curtain rings or plastic lids with the center cut out and attach different colors of cloth ribbon, wrapping-paper ribbon, or streamers. Put on some music, like Jim Gill's song "I Changed My Mind," and have children create dance steps and use their ribbon circles.

Instrument
Castanets

Supplies:
- ▶ Foam sheets, cut into 2-inch-by-4-inch strips: 1 strip for each child
- ▶ Buttons or bottle caps: 2 for each child
- ▶ Tacky glue
- ▶ Markers or crayons

Directions:
- ▶ Before the program cut the foam sheets into strips.
- ▶ Have children decorate the foam strips.

- ▶ Have adults use tacky glue to attach a button at the top and bottom of one side of the length of strip.
- ▶ Once the glue is dry, have children fold the foam in half so that the two buttons click against each other.
- ▶ Children can practice playing the castanets like Fritz the goat.

BONUS BOOKS

Ballroom Bonanza, by Nina Rycroft and Stephen Harris and illustrated by Nina Rycroft (Abrams Books for Young Readers, 2009).

The alphabet book features dancing animals: donkeys that disco, impalas that tango, monkeys that mamba, and turkeys that twist, just to name a few. Some of the dances are easily recognizable, like line dancing, but others like the watusi might not be familiar to children. At the end of the story, monkeys have hidden the band's instruments, and children can look through the book again to find all twenty-six instruments in the illustrations. Children learn the names of various instruments as they search for the hidden images.

Conejito: A Folktale from Panama, by Margaret Read MacDonald and illustrated by Geraldo Valério (August House LittleFolk, 2006).

Conejito leaves home to spend time with his aunt, Tía Mónica. He dances on his way to her home. He also runs into Señor Zorro, Señor León, and Señor Tigre, who all want to eat him for lunch. Conejito says they should wait until he comes back, because Tía Mónica will feed him lots of food and fatten him up. Luckily, Conejito's aunt comes up with a clever plan to get Conejito home safely. While Conejito dances, he sings a short, catchy song about his aunt. The music for the song is included at the end of the book.

Dogs Don't Do Ballet, by Anna Kemp and illustrated by Sara Ogilvie (Simon & Schuster Books for Young Readers, 2010).

A young girl's dog, Biff, has an extraordinary skill. He dances ballet. The girl's father says that's impossible, but Biff proves him and everyone else wrong in spectacular dancing fashion.

Every Cowgirl Needs Dancing Boots, by Rebecca Janni and illustrated by Lynne Avril (Dutton Children's Books, 2011).

Nellie Sue has new dancing boots but no friends with whom to dance. She invites the ballerina neighbor girls to her barnyard bash in the hopes that she will find a dance partner and maybe even a friend. Will her party be a success, or will an untimely lemonade spill ruin the day?

How Do You Wokka-Wokka? **by Elizabeth Bluemle and illustrated by Randy Cecil (Candlewick Press, 2009).**

It's a new day, perfect to dance and "wokka" in your own special way. A boy asks the neighborhood children how they "wokka-wokka." Each one demonstrates a new approach. In the end, children and adults alike join in a neighborhood dance party. After reading the story, encourage children to show their own way to "wokka-wokka." If children can't think of a dance style, encourage them to dance like one of the characters in the book or to brainstorm types of dance like the cat, a floating leaf, or the bicycle.

***Miss Lina's Ballerinas*, by Grace Maccarone and illustrated by Christine Davenier (Feiwel and Friends, 2010).**

Christina, Edwina, Sabrina, Justina, Katrina, Bettina, Marina, and Nina have a passion for dance. They dance all day, and they dance with everything they do. They dance four by four, and they dance two by two. When a new girl joins the class, they aren't sure how to dance with nine. Miss Lina, the dance instructor, has an idea that saves the day.

***Naughty Toes*, by Ann Bonwill and illustrated by Teresa Murfin (Tiger Tales, 2011).**

Chloe isn't like all the other ballerinas. She wears colorful leotards, and her hair escapes her bun. She dances with more enthusiasm than grace, much to her dance instructor's dismay. Madame Mina says Chloe has "naughty toes" and assigns her a dance role as a rock. Mr. Tiempo, the accompanist, understands Chloe better than anyone else and has a special surprise for her—tap shoes.

***Tallulah's Tutu*, by Marilyn Singer and illustrated by Alexandra Boiger (Clarion Books, 2011).**

Tallulah thinks that all she needs to be a ballerina is a tutu. Her mom signs her up for dance classes, and at each class Tallulah believes she is the most talented dancer and surely is ready for her tutu. Her teacher doesn't agree and reminds her about the importance of practicing. Tallulah quits dance in a fit of frustration, but she can't stop thinking about it. Maybe the tutu isn't the most important thing.

***Tutus Aren't My Style*, by Linda Skeers and illustrated by Anne Wilsdorf (Dial Books for Young Readers, 2010).**

Emma traps frogs and wears cowboy boots, but she doesn't know what to do with the ballerina outfit her uncle sent her. Neighbors tell her dancers are light on their feet and effortless. Emma tries but can't quite get the knack of being a ballerina until she creates her own dancing rules.

BONUS TRACKS

Jim Gill frequently incorporates movement into his music, and many of his songs are perfect for this theme. *Jim Gill's Irrational Anthem and More Salutes to Nonsense* has several: "I'll Spell It out for You," "Buffet Ballet," and "The Dance-Along Gong Song" (Jim Gill Music, 2001). *Jim Gill Sings Moving Rhymes for Modern Times* has the song "Jim Gill's Groove" (Jim Gill Music, 2005). The "Silly Dance Contest" is found on the recording *Jim Gill Sings the Sneezing Song and Other Contagious Tunes* (Jim Gill Music, 1993). "List of Dances" and "Let's Dance Now" are found on *Jim Gill Makes It Noisy in Boise, Idaho* (Jim Gill Music, 1995).

"Ants in My Pants," from the recording *Grandkid Rock*, by Daddy a Go Go (Boyd's Tone Records, 2011).
Follow along and dance as instructed to this rocking, rhyming song about the need to boogie.

"Cherry Pants," from the recording *Rhythm Train*, by Leslie Bixler and Chad Smith and featuring Dick Van Dyke (Leslie Bixler, 2010).
There are certain objects and clothing needed when doing different activities, like practicing yoga or playing tennis. When it's time to dance, the object needed is cherry pants. Whenever cherry pants are mentioned, dance quickly and energetically.

"Do the Walk," from the recording *Imagination Generation*, by David Kisor (Growing Sound, 2010).
Listen to the song's directions and walk, roll, and wiggle. The second time around, use your imagination and creativity and decide how you want to walk, roll, and wiggle. Finish with a dance that is all your own.

***Everyone Loves to Dance!* by Aaron Nigel Smith (Music for Little People, 2010).**
Dance along by swaying, bouncing, and jumping to the rhythm of "Everyone Loves to Dance." Listen to "Can You Dance?" and decide if the different parts of your body, like your nose, stomach, and fingers, can dance.

"Freezedance," by Tom Freund and Friends, from the recording *Kids World Party* (Putumayo World Music, 2011).
Get your dance groove on until you hear the word *freeze*.

"I Can Dance," from the recording *My Name Is Chicken Joe*, by Trout Fishing in America (Folle Avoine Productions, 2009).

Don't be shy. Hit the floor and dance!

"I Really Love to Dance," from the recording *The Best of the Laurie Berkner Band*, by the Laurie Berkner Band (Two Tomatoes Records, 2010), or from the recording *Love and Peace: Greatest Hits for Kids* (Music for Little People, 2010).

Nothing quite compares to the love of dancing.

"Let's Dance," from the recording *Oh Lucky Day!* by Lucky Diaz and the Family Jam Band (Rainy Day Dimes Music, 2011).

Dancing is contagious. Join in and dance along wherever you are.

"Let's Samba," from the recording *Rocketship Run*, by the Laurie Berkner Band (Two Tomatoes Records, 2008).

Practice your samba by moving your feet to the song.

***Ranky Tanky*, by Rani Arbo and Daisy Mayhem (Mayhem Music, 2010).**

Free-style dance to *Ranky Tanky* and point to the different body parts mentioned. Practice the steps to the "Tennessee Wig Walk" and dance like a duck.

CHAPTER 7
A SOUND HULLABALOO

In this program children learn about the science of sound and the noises that surround them. Begin by having participants close their eyes and listen as you make a sound with an object. Once they think they know what the sound is, have them raise their hand. After making the same sound a couple of times, let children guess what they heard. Repeat with several other sounds. Examples of sounds to use are jiggling coins, stapling a piece of paper, and opening a soda can.

After the activity, ask children if they know how their ears work. What about sound waves? What makes music different from noise? Share some facts from a nonfiction book such as *Sound: Music to Our Ears*, by Emily Sohn and Diane Bair (Norwood House Press, 2011).

PROGRAM PLAYLIST
- ▶ Opening Song: "Making Good Noise," from the recording *Making Good Noise*, by Tom Chapin
- ▶ Book: *Ol' Bloo's Boogie-Woogie Band and Blues Ensemble*, by Jan Huling and illustrated by Henri Sørensen
- ▶ Song: "N-O-I-S-E"
- ▶ Book: *Holler Loudly*, by Cynthia Leitich Smith and illustrated by Barry Gott
- ▶ Song: "Yodel Lady Who," from the recording *Kid's Country Song and Dance: Action, Sing-Along, Hoe-Down Fun!* by the Learning Station

- ▶ Book: *The Great Monster Hunt*, by Norbert Landa and illustrated by Tim Warnes
- ▶ Song: "The Music Song," from the recording *Radio Wayne*, by Wayne Brady
- ▶ Book: *The Gingerbread Girl Goes Animal Crackers*, by Lisa Campbell Ernst
- ▶ Activity: Water Glass Scale
- ▶ Musical Instrument: Guitar

Opening Song

"Making Good Noise," from the recording *Making Good Noise*, by Tom Chapin (Sundance Music, 2003).
Children can make a hullabaloo by using their body as an instrument. Each verse has new actions like snapping fingers and clapping hands.

Book

***Ol' Bloo's Boogie-Woogie Band and Blues Ensemble*, by Jan Huling and illustrated by Henri Sørensen (Peachtree Publishers, 2010).**
Ol' Bloo Donkey, Gnarly Dog, One-Eyed Lemony Cat, and Rusty Red Rooster leave home when their owners stop appreciating them. They find one another and head to New Orleans to form a band and play their own special brand of music. On the way they discover a house with three people and a lot of food. The people don't look too friendly, but the animals decide to sing in the hopes that the strangers (who are robbers!) will share their food. Their singing, though a pleasing sound to the four animals, in actuality sounds so discordant and shrill that it sends the robbers scrambling out of the house and running for safety. Will the robbers come back? Will the animals be able to play their music in New Orleans? This entertaining version of the folktale of the Bremen Town Musicians has a wonderful Louisiana flavor. Divide your audience into four groups and assign each group an animal. Have the groups practice what they think that animal sounds like. Then when it is their turn to participate, they can join in with the loud obnoxious singing.

Song

"N-O-I-S-E" (sung to the tune "B-I-N-G-O")
Ol' Bloo's band sings a song and
NOISE is its name-o
N-O-I-S-E
N-O-I-S-E
N-O-I-S-E
And NOISE is its name-o.

Sing the song again, but this time take out the letter *N* and replace it with a clap, a stamp, or a donkey's hee-haw.

Ol' Bloo's band sings a song and
NOISE is its name-o
(Clap) O-I-S-E
(Clap) O-I-S-E
(Clap) O-I-S-E
And NOISE is its name-o.

Continue in this manner until the whole word is replaced with a series of claps, stamps, or hee-haws.

Book

Holler Loudly, by Cynthia Leitich Smith and illustrated by Barry Gott (Dutton Children's Books, 2010).
Every once in a blue moon, a Loudly baby is born who is just plain loud! Holler is that baby. Every time he gets excited, his voice rises and items like chalk break. Holler annoys his classmates and the townspeople with his ever-present loud voice until a tornado roars into town. Can Holler face down the tornado and save the town?

Song

"Yodel Lady Who," from the recording *Kid's Country Song and Dance: Action, Sing-Along, Hoe-Down Fun!* by the Learning Station (Monopoli and the Learning Station, 2009).
Follow up on the previous book with an entertaining song that teaches children step by step how to yodel. If you don't have this song, try Jim Gill's

song "Yodeling," from the recording *Jim Gill's Irrational Anthem and More Salutes to Nonsense*, by Jim Gill (Jim Gill Music, 2001).

Book

The Great Monster Hunt, by Norbert Landa and illustrated by Tim Warnes (Good Books, 2010).

Duck hears a sound from underneath his bed and is so scared he rushes to Pig for help. In describing the sound to his friend, he unconsciously adds on to it. Pig thinks the sound is quite scary, and they need Bear's strength to help. In this game of telephone the noise progressively gets louder and scarier as each animal shares the story while seeking help from another. Together the animals come up with a plan to catch the monster, but they are surprised to see what the "monster" really is.

Song

"The Music Song," from the recording *Radio Wayne*, by Wayne Brady (Walt Disney Records, 2011).

Children create music as Brady encourages them to clap, stamp, and sing to this entertaining tune.

Book

The Gingerbread Girl Goes Animal Crackers, by Lisa Campbell Ernst (Dutton Children's Books, 2011).

For the Gingerbread Girl's birthday, she is given a birthday present of animal crackers. As soon as she opens the box, the race is on! The animal crackers run off singing a song that challenges anyone to catch them. As the animals race through the area passing farm animals and children, each type of animal cracker sings its own fierce song until they all reach the fox. The fox promises he can help the animal crackers cross the water safely, and they believe him. Once they are in the middle of the lake, they realize that the fox has lied. This story has lots of opportunity for children to sing along and make animal noises.

Activity
Water Glass Scale

For this activity share some science experiments about sound. For example, you can create a musical scale using the directions found in *A Project Guide to Sound*, by Colleen Kessler (Mitchell Lane Publishers, 2012). For this science experiment you will need eight identical glasses filled with varying amounts of water and a metal spoon. When you tap the metal spoon against the individual glasses, you will hear different notes.

Musical Instrument
Guitar

Supplies:
- ▶ Shoe boxes: 1 per child
- ▶ Rubber bands: 4–5 per child
- ▶ Pencils or craft sticks: 1 for each child
- ▶ Decorating materials

Directions:
- ▶ Shoe boxes are the hardest items to get for this craft, so start gathering early or ask participants to bring their own.
- ▶ The shoe box represents the body of the guitar. Before the program, cut a hole in the center of the top of each box.
- ▶ Have children decorate the boxes.
- ▶ Give children rubber bands so that they can put them around the box, crossing over the hole like guitar strings would.
- ▶ Have them wedge a pencil between the rubber bands and the bottom of the box lid. This creates a bridge.
- ▶ To increase the tension of the rubber bands and keep the pencil in place, children can wrap each rubber band around the pencil. As the rubber bands tighten or loosen, their sound will change.
- ▶ Have children experiment with strumming or plucking the rubber bands. Share some facts about rubber bands and vibrations from the book *Investigating Sound*, by Sally M. Walker (Lerner Publications Company, 2012).

Activity
Water Glass Scale

For this activity share some science experiments about sound. For example, you can create a musical scale using the directions found in *A Project Guide to Sound*, by Colleen Kessler (Mitchell Lane Publishers, 2012). For this science experiment you will need eight identical glasses filled with varying amounts of water and a metal spoon. When you tap the metal spoon against the individual glasses, you will hear different notes.

Musical Instrument
Guitar

Supplies:
- ▶ Shoe boxes: 1 per child
- ▶ Rubber bands: 4–5 per child
- ▶ Pencils or craft sticks: 1 for each child
- ▶ Decorating materials

Directions:
- ▶ Shoe boxes are the hardest items to get for this craft, so start gathering early or ask participants to bring their own.
- ▶ The shoe box represents the body of the guitar. Before the program, cut a hole in the center of the top of each box.
- ▶ Have children decorate the boxes.
- ▶ Give children rubber bands so that they can put them around the box, crossing over the hole like guitar strings would.
- ▶ Have them wedge a pencil between the rubber bands and the bottom of the box lid. This creates a bridge.
- ▶ To increase the tension of the rubber bands and keep the pencil in place, children can wrap each rubber band around the pencil. As the rubber bands tighten or loosen, their sound will change.
- ▶ Have children experiment with strumming or plucking the rubber bands. Share some facts about rubber bands and vibrations from the book *Investigating Sound*, by Sally M. Walker (Lerner Publications Company, 2012).

BONUS BOOKS

Bedtime Hullabaloo, **by David Conway and illustrated by Charles Fuge (Walker & Company, 2010).**

While getting ready for bed, a leopard hears a strange sound. As he searches for the source of the hullabaloo, other savanna animals join him. To make the story interactive, create signs for the different sounds and words that repeat throughout the story. Encourage children to join in when you hold up the appropriate sign.

Crash Bang Donkey! **by Jill Newton (Albert Whitman & Company, 2010).**

Crash Bang Donkey adores playing music, but his music prevents Farmer Gruff from napping. After spending all hours of the day chasing crows out of his field, Farmer Gruff wants some peace and sleep. The banging and the crashing are just too much! Donkey leaves and starts playing his music on the other side of the farm. That's when the animals realize that Donkey's special brand of music scares the crows away. Maybe, just maybe, Farmer Gruff will learn to like Donkey's noise.

Investigating Sound, **by Sally M. Walker (Lerner Publications Company, 2012).**

Use simple experiments to demonstrate the properties of sound. Most of the experiments can be done with items around the house like rubber bands, a garden hose, and a metal spoon and pan.

Jackhammer Sam, **by Peter Mandel and illustrated by David Catrow (Roaring Brook Press, 2011).**

An enthusiastic construction worker named Jackhammer Sam shares his bubbling excitement for the important job that he does and the music he makes blasting concrete. Catrow's humorous illustrations complement the text of the story. Jackhammer Sam sings a song throughout the story that always begins with the same two words and follows with different ways to describe his work with the jackhammer. Afterward children can use the same format and create their own construction song.

The Loud Book! **by Deborah Underwood and illustrated by Renata Liwska (Houghton Mifflin Books for Children, 2011).**

In the companion to *The Quiet Book* (Houghton Mifflin Books for Children, 2010), Underwood describes a variety of loud sounds from alarm clocks to burps to thunderstorms. Between the descriptive language and the illustrations, this book thoroughly explores the concepts of loudness and noise.

Monkey with a Tool Belt and the Noisy Problem, by Chris Monroe (Carolrhoda Books, 2009).

Monkey hears a noise and is determined to find the source and fix it with his handy tool belt. He looks all over but can't find the cause, until he throws something down the laundry shoot. Someone is stuck, and children will be surprised to find out what animal is making that strange noise.

Music, by Dan Green (Kingfisher, 2011).

This book provides a little bit of information about a lot of different topics. Learn about the components of music: pitch, tempo, and rhythm. Find out what notes, rests, and scales are. Included are brief overviews of types of instruments and genres of music.

A Project Guide to Sound, by Colleen Kessler (Mitchell Lane Publishers, 2012).

How is sound produced? How is noise different from music? Does sound travel faster through gases, liquids, or solids? Learn about the science of sound through facts and experiments. Some experiments use easily accessible materials like tracing paper and poster board to create a sonic boom or straws to learn about vibration. The book has a lot of ideas you can use to set up several experiment stations to explore qualities of sound.

Sound: Music to Our Ears, by Emily Sohn and Diane Bair (Norwood House, 2011).

Use this book to convey information about sound waves and pitch. The book also contains a variety of experiments that you can employ to introduce the theme or that you can intersperse throughout the program.

The Squeaky Door, retold by Margaret Read MacDonald and illustrated by Mary Newell DePalma (HarperCollins Publishers, 2006).

A squeaky door coupled with a dark bedroom scare a little boy when he stays at Grandma's house. To calm his fear, Grandma puts the boy to bed with his cat. When the squeaky door scares the boy and the cat, she brings in the dog. So starts a chain of events. Can Grandma find the key to solving the little boy's fear? You can extend the story by adding more animals or create a twist by having children suggest other things that can make a scary noise at night: a loose floorboard or a branch hitting the window. As with many of MacDonald's stories, there are participatory options for the crowd. Children can make animal sounds, create the sound of the squeaky door, or repeat several phrases.

The String Family in Harmony! **by Trisha Speed Shaskan and illustrated by Robert Meganck (Picture Window Books, 2011).**
Learn the similarities and differences of the violin, the viola, the harp, the guitar, and the double bass. Share some facts about the string family when introducing the guitar craft.

Stringed Instruments, **by Anita Ganeri (Smart Apple Media, 2012).**
The book talks about stringed instruments like the cello, the lute, the ukulele, and the guitar. It has facts, pictures, and diagrams of the instruments to help explain what they look like and how they work. It also explains the concept of vibration and how vibrating strings create music.

Too Much Noise in the Library, **by Susan Margaret Chapman and illustrated by Abby Carter (UpstartBooks, 2010).**
Ms. Reade's school media center is abuzz with activity and the noise of books sliding through the return slot, laughing kids, and tapping computer keys. When the mayor visits, he thinks it is much too noisy and shuts off the computers, locks up the books, and shoos the children out of the library. Once the computers are off, the books put away, and the library empty of children, it is quiet just as the mayor likes. What will the mayor do when he finds it too quiet? This story has seven specific sounds in the library. One quick way to make the story interactive is to give children a sound effect they are responsible for making when the time comes.

The Violin and Other Stringed Instruments, **by Rita Storey (Smart Apple Media, 2010).**
What is a violin made of, and how does it make the sounds that we hear? What is a sitar and a bouzouki? Read the book to find out these answers and more interesting facts about string instruments. This book is one in a series called Let's Make Music.

BONUS TRACKS

Jim Gill Makes It Noisy in Boise, Idaho, **by Jim Gill (Jim Gill Music, 1995).**
Join Jim Gill and his band and make some noise by clapping and snapping fingers to the song "The Night We Made It Noisy in Boise, Idaho." Listen to "The Sound Effects Song," and hear the many sounds of home. Children can join in and make those same sounds.

"Loud and Quiet," from the recording *Sing Along!* by Caspar Babypants (Aurora Elephant Music, 2011).

Explore concepts of loud and quiet by having children make animal noises loudly and quietly.

"Loud/Quiet," from the songbook and CD *Blue Moo: 17 Jukebox Hits from Way Back Never*, by Sandra Boynton (Workman Publishing, 2007).

The book *Blue Moo* has an accompanying CD. Listen to moments of loud and quiet music.

"My Aunt Came Back," from the recording *Kid's Country Song and Dance: Action, Sing-Along, Hoe-Down Fun!* by the Learning Station (Monopoli and the Learning Station, 2009).

In an echo song that rhymes, an aunt travels to different areas and brings back objects that rhyme with those places. Create additional verses with children by having them come up with the names of places to visit and souvenirs that rhyme with those places. Possibilities include New York and stork, and Tennessee and tea.

"What's That Sound?" from the recording *Make Your Own Someday: Silly Songs for the Shorter Set*, by the Jimmies (Pluckypea Records, 2007).

What do different instruments like the triangle, the Chinese gong, the piano, and the banjo sound like?

CHAPTER 8
MUSICAL POTPOURRI

ne of the exciting aspects of music is its variety: country, rock and roll, classical, hip-hop, zydeco, and so much more. The books and activities in this chapter explore the richness and range of music. As an introduction ask children to list different genres of music. Then share a couple short clips of various styles and see if they can name what type of music it is.

PROGRAM PLAYLIST

▶ Opening Song: "Let's Shake," by Dan Zanes and Friends, from the recording *Rock & Roll Playground*

▶ Book: *Rock 'n' Roll Mole*, by Carolyn Crimi and illustrated by Lynn Munsinger

▶ Song: "Put Your Finger in the Air," from the recording *For Kids and Just Plain Folks*, by Pete Seeger

▶ Book: *The Middle-Child Blues*, by Kristyn Crow and illustrated by David Catrow

▶ Song: "Country Medley," from the recording *Kid's Country Song and Dance: Action, Sing-Along, Hoe-Down Fun!* by the Learning Station

▶ Book: *She'll Be Coming 'Round the Mountain*, by Jonathan Emmett and illustrated by Deborah Allwright

▶ Song: "Twist and Shout," from the recording *Buckwheat Zydeco's Bayou Boogie*, by Buckwheat Zydeco

▶ Book: *Cool Daddy Rat*, by Kristyn Crow and illustrated by Mike Lester

▶ Activity: Musical Art
▶ Musical Instrument: Spoons

Opening Song

"Let's Shake," by Dan Zanes and Friends, from the recording *Rock & Roll Playground* **(Putumayo World Music, 2010).**

Dan Zanes and Friends encourage children to shake, twist, and do other dances. The recording has several other action songs that are also good to use. Practice your hand jive with the song "Willie and the Hand Jive," by Taj Mahal and Linda Tillery. "Jump Up (It's a Good Day)," by Brady Rymer and the Little Band That Could extols everyone to jump up and enjoy the day. There are also a couple traditional folk songs set to rock accompaniment, including "Row, Row, Row Your Boat," by Charity and the JAMband, which has movements that children can act out.

Book

Rock 'n' Roll Mole, **by Carolyn Crimi and illustrated by Lynn Munsinger (Dial Books for Young Readers, 2011).**

Rock 'n' Roll Mole looks the part with a leather jacket and shades, but his acute stage fright keeps him from sharing his music. Can he get over his fear to help his friend Pig at the talent show?

Song

"Put Your Finger in the Air," from the recording *For Kids and Just Plain Folks*, **by Pete Seeger (Sony Music Entertainment, 1997).**

Seeger recorded a live version of this folk song. Children are encouraged to put their finger in the air, on their chin, on their toe, and on other body parts.

Book

The Middle-Child Blues, **by Kristyn Crow and illustrated by David Catrow (G. P. Putnam's Sons, 2009).**

For all the middle children out there, Lee strikes up a blues song about being forgotten, overlooked, and being too little and too big all at the same time.

Song

"Country Medley," from the recording *Kid's Country Song and Dance: Action, Sing-Along, Hoe-Down Fun!* **by the Learning Station (Monopoli and the Learning Station, 2009).**
In "Country Medley," different country songs like "Old Gray Mare," "Home on the Range," "Polly Wolly Doodle," and "Paw Paw Patch" are introduced. One way to make the medley interactive is to have a different activity for each song. For example, children can clap their hands for one song and pat their knees for another, or they can snap their fingers or march in place.

Book

She'll Be Coming 'Round the Mountain, **by Jonathan Emmett and illustrated by Deborah Allwright (Atheneum Books for Young Readers, 2006).**
Who's that coming around the mountain? A pink-pajama-wearing, energetic little girl gallops into town. Each verse of this entertaining folk song has an action associated with it, helping children participate in the storytelling.

Song

"Twist and Shout," from the recording *Buckwheat Zydeco's Bayou Boogie,* **by Buckwheat Zydeco (Musical Kidz, 2010).**
Use the twist to introduce children to the musical style zydeco. A few other action songs include "Loop De Loop," "Loco-Motion," and "Hokey Pokey."

Book

Cool Daddy Rat, **by Kristyn Crow and illustrated by Mike Lester (G. P. Putnam's Sons, 2008).**
Ace's father, Cool Daddy Rat, plays jazz beats on his bass throughout the city rooftops to Times Square. One night Ace hides in his father's instrument case. Cool Daddy Rat discovers his son and lets him stay and see him perform. At one of his gigs, he realizes that his son has a musical gift too: he can scat. This book is an engaging way to introduce children to singing scat.

Activity
Musical Art

Give each child a piece of paper and crayons or markers. Explain that classical music often tells a story. Play a short piece like "Elephants," from Camille Saint-Saëns's *The Carnival of the Animals* (Alfred A. Knopf, 2010). For other options, check out *Piano Music for Children* (Dal Segno, 2009). Ask children to draw a picture inspired by the music.

Musical Instrument
Spoons

Supplies:

- ▶ Pairs of identical spoons: 1 set for each child (giving away spoons at a program may seem like an expensive proposition, but don't forget that thrift stores, dollar stores, and garage sales can be great places to get inexpensive musical supplies. You can also ask participants to bring in two matching spoons for the activity if you aren't sure that you will have enough)
- ▶ Cardboard
- ▶ Masking tape

How to Play Spoons, by Cindy Brown

Before the program teach yourself how to play spoons. If you search for "playing spoons" on YouTube, a variety of how-to videos can be found.

Choose a pair of identical spoons. Metal, plastic, and wooden spoons all work. Choose spoons that fit best in your hand or that make the sound you like. Start off with a teaspoon size, though.

Hold the bottom spoon facedown between your pointer and middle finger.

Hold the top spoon face up between your pointer finger and thumb. The spoons should be back to back.

Press the ends of the spoons into the palm of your hand and press your thumb down on the spoon handle for stability. There should be a little bit of space between the spoons. That is the hardest part!

Basic move: Hit the spoons on your knee to hear the "click." Put your free hand up and over the hand with the spoons. Hit the spoons on your knee and let them come up to hit the palm of your free hand. Practice this until you get the feel and can do a steady beat. When you feel comfortable and the spoons don't fall out of your hand, try adding a roll.

Roll: To add a little pizzazz, open your free hand, spreading your fingers far apart. Hold this hand vertically in the air. Take your "spoon hand" and allow the spoon to hit each finger, bouncing down your free hand. Finish this move with a hit on your knee for the last beat.

Directions:
▶ Some children will be able to hold the spoons between their fingers and play them. For others who might find this difficult, you can modify the spoons by placing cardboard between the spoon handles and wrapping both the cardboard and the spoons in masking tape. You will need to add enough cardboard so that the top of the spoons are slightly apart but will still hit each other when you tap your spoons on your knee. The modified version of spoons is easier for children to hold.

▶ Show children how to keep a steady rhythm by tapping the spoons on their knees. Once they are comfortable with that move, have them put their free hand above their knee and bring their spoons down to tap their knee and up to tap the palm of their hand, back and forth.

▶ Then play the song "Country Medley" and invite them to tap along.

BONUS BOOKS

The Composer Is Dead, **by Lemony Snicket and illustrated by Carson Ellis (HarperCollins Publishers, 2009).**

An inspector investigates the death of a composer. He interrogates the instruments in the string section, the brass section, the woodwind section, and the percussion section. Use this story to introduce the different families and individual instruments that make up an orchestra. The included CD has musical accompaniment that illustrates the story. Although the CD is almost an hour long, you can share the story and then play some of the selections as background music while children are doing other activities.

Cool Country Music: Create and Appreciate What Makes Music Great! **by Mary Lindeen (Abdo Publishing Company, 2008).**

Discover the different types of country music like western swing, bluegrass, and Tex-Mex. Find lists of country music stars and songs, as well as instruments like banjos and harmonicas that are used in country music. The book suggests several activities, including crafting a banjo, composing a country song, and dancing the Texas two-step. Additional books in the Cool Music series are *Cool Classical Music, Cool Hip-Hop Music, Cool Latin Music, Cool Reggae Music,* and *Cool Rock Music.*

The Django, **by Levi Pinfold (Templar Books, 2010).**

A magical trickster creature named the Django causes problems for a young boy. Despite the boy's insistence that he shouldn't play his father's banjo, the Django does it anyway and breaks it. He plays tricks on the boy when he is out in public, messing up the boy's words and causing him to dance around a farm and create a ruckus that disturbs the animals. Fed up, the boy tells the Django to leave and never come back. The Django disappears, but over time the boy misses his friend. When his dad gives him a banjo, the boy has a plan to do something he knows the Django will like.

The inspiration for this story came from Jean "Django" Reinhardt, a jazz-banjo performer from France.

Duke Ellington's Nutcracker Suite, by Anna Harwell Celenza and illustrated by Don Tate (Charlesbridge, 2011).

A friend encouraged Duke Ellington to remake the well-known *Nutcracker Suite* ballet with a jazz twist. The book shows the process he went through with his band to create a new version of a holiday classic. Although the book is a bit text heavy to use as a read-aloud in a program, it is good to share in a classroom setting to talk about different versions of the *Nutcracker Suite* or bits and pieces of the story can be used to introduce children to Duke Ellington. The book comes with a CD of Ellington's *Nutcracker Suite.* One activity would be to play his version of a piece like "The Volga Vouty" and compare it with Tchaikovsky's "Russian Dance."

Ella Bella Ballerina and Swan Lake, by James Mayhew (Barron's, 2011).

In a picture book introduction to the ballet *Swan Lake*, by Peter Tchaikovsky, Ella Bella's ballet teacher shares the story of *Swan Lake*. While Ella Bella is dancing alone to the instructor's music box, she suddenly finds herself in the story interacting with Odette, the Swan Princess, and Odile, the evil sorceress. Mayhew has two other books in the Ella Bella series, *Ella Bella Ballerina and Cinderella* (Barron's, 2009) and *Ella Bella Ballerina and the Sleeping Beauty* (Barron's, 2008). Use this series to introduce children to classical ballet.

Hip Hop Dog, by Chris Raschka and illustrated by Vladimir Radunsky (HarperCollins Publishers, 2010).

A lonely dog raps about his feelings of being on his own and unloved. The process of creating music makes him feel better. He realizes that it might be okay, even cool, to be Hip Hop Dog.

Jake the Philharmonic Dog, by Karen LeFrak and illustrated by Marcin Baranski (Walker and Company, 2006).

Richie, principal stagehand, discovers Jake, a dog who sings when he barks. When Richie takes him to work, Jack "woofs" to the notes of the flute, "ruffs" to the honk of a French horn, and cries at the sound of the thunderous drums. Only the strings quiet his panic. When he plays with a stick that he finds, the audience and conductor are in for a surprise.

Jazzmatazz! by Stephanie Calmenson and illustrated by Bruce Degen (HarperCollins Publishers, 2008).

A mouse tiptoes across the piano keys, creating a jazz song. In join the dog, the cat, the bird, the fish, and finally the baby in a family "jazzmatazz."

John Denver's Grandma's Feather Bed, **adapted and illustrated by Christopher Canyon (Dawn Publications, 2007).**

In the song "Grandma's Feather Bed," Denver reminisces about visiting Grandma and sleeping in an enormous bed with kids and dogs and a pig. It's a celebration of fun family times. The book includes information about John Denver and his friend Jim Connor, who wrote the song. It also comes with a CD of John Denver performing the piece. If you enjoy the story, check out *John Denver's Take Me Home, Country Roads*, also adapted and illustrated by Christopher Canyon (Dawn Publications, 2005).

One Love, **based on the song by Bob Marley, adapted by Cedella Marley and illustrated by Vanessa Brantley-Newton (Chronicle Books, 2011).**

Join the joyful celebration of family and community working in harmony to create a neighborhood park.

One Shoe Blues, Starring B. B. King: Storybook, Song, Movie Short, **by Sandra Boynton (Workman Publishing, 2009).**

In typical hilarious Boynton fashion, the author introduces children to blues and B. B. King with an entertaining movie short. B. B. King has lost one of his green shoes and sings the blues. The other actors in the movie are sock puppets. The book contains a DVD of the movie short, the story with photos, and sheet music for the song "One Shoe Blues."

Passing the Music Down, **by Sarah Sullivan and illustrated by Barry Root (Candlewick Press, 2011).**

Sullivan writes a fictional story based on the real friendship between fiddlers Melvin Wine and Jake Krack. As a young boy Jake learned from a fiddle master how to play folk songs that many people don't know anymore. Melvin taught Jake not only how to play folk music but also how to pass it on.

Symphony City, **by Amy Martin (McSweeney's McMullens, 2011).**

In the hustle of a packed subway, a young girl loses her adult companion. She listens to the sound of music and pursues it, walking out of the subway and into the city. From street musicians playing the flute and piano to a French-horn player practicing by the window and electric guitarists jamming underneath the streetlights, music and musicians are everywhere. Martin is a graphic artist, and the illustrations are the true focus of this book. Nature, music, and cityscape are intertwined in the artwork. When sharing the book, ask children to look for the instruments in each of the illustrations. Afterward, see how many of the instruments they remember and have them make a list. If you know people who can play the instruments highlighted in the book, consider asking them to come to the program and talk about their instruments and then briefly play so the children can connect the instrument with the sound it makes. If you don't have access to musicians or the time to invite them to a program, use the book *Those Amazing Musical Instruments!*, by Genevieve Helsby (Sourcebooks Jabberwocky, 2007), which has a CD-ROM that includes sound clips of many instruments. Introduce the instruments by playing selections and sharing pictures and fun facts about each one.

This Jazz Man, by Karen Ehrhardt and illustrated by R. G. Roth (Live Oak Media, 2010).

Sung to the counting tune "This Old Man," the story introduces children to jazz music and the instruments used. At the end of the book, nine jazz musicians are mentioned, with biographical information about each one. Harcourt published the original book in 2006. This version, by Live Oak Media, is accompanied with a CD that includes James "D-Train" Williams as the narrator and fantastic jazz accompaniment.

BONUS TRACKS

American Folk, Game & Activity Songs for Children, by Pete Seeger (Smithsonian Folkways Recordings, 2000).

One of the best-known folk singers, Pete Seeger has several CDs for young children. In "Frog Went A-Courting" he encourages children to join in and repeat certain parts of the song. Before playing "Jim Along Josie," have children form a circle and then listen to the lyrics and do the actions as described. Children will walk, run, crawl, tiptoe, and more. In "Clap Your Hands" children clap their hands, stamp their feet, and nod their head.

The Animal Faire, by Tony Robinson (Tony Robinson Music, 2011).

This musical CD has songs from the perspective of different animals. The rock song "Dirty Dog Day" is performed from the viewpoint of dingos. The Creek Critters perform a bluesy "Cookie Stew." The snakes rap in "Rattle and Hiss."

Beethoven's Wig 3, by Richard Perlmutter (Rounder Records, 2005).

On this CD, classical pieces are redone with new lyrics. Each piece features an orchestra instrument. For example, "Silver Winds" highlights the flute using music from "Dance of the Reed Flutes" from the *Nutcracker Suite*, and "Where, Oh Where" highlights the clarinet and oboe using "Funeral March of a Marionette."

Blue Moo: 17 Jukebox Hits from Way Back Never, by Sandra Boynton (Workman Publishing, 2007).

Boynton has written a collection of songs that feel like they came out of the 1950s and 1960s. Included with the songbook is a CD with performances by well-known musicians like Neil Sedaka, Patti LuPone, and Davy Jones of the Monkees. A few of my favorites include "Gorilla Song," performed by Sha Na Na; "One Shoe Blues," performed by B. B. King; and "Big Band Sound," performed by John Ondrasik of Five for Fighting. Boynton illustrates each song with her trademark characters. She also includes lyrics, music, and information about the performers.

The Body Rocks: Songs about the Human Body, **by Marc "Doc" Dauer (Rounder Records, 2010).**

Dauer has created rock songs about the brain, sight, heart, and even why pee is important. Guest artists like Liz Phair, Pete Yorn, and Minnie Driver join in the fun.

Buzz Buzz, **by Laurie Berkner (Two Tomatoes Records, 1998).**

Berkner performs two American folk songs: "The Erie Canal," a song about barges and shipping, and "I've Been Working on the Railroad," describing rail work.

"Chicken Joe," from the recording *My Name Is Chicken Joe*, **by Trout Fishing in America (Folle Avoine Productions, 2009).**

Each verse features an animal with a funny name, like a cat named Chicken Joe and a dog named Miss Kitty. The song has a folk-rock feel to it.

Dog Train: Deluxe Illustrated Lyrics Book of the Unpredictable Rock-and-Roll Journey, **by Sandra Boynton (Workman Publishing, 2005).**

Boynton's songbook includes funny and entertaining lyrics that are performed on the accompanying CD by musicians like Alison Krauss, Hootie and the Blowfish, and Spin Doctors. She even has Kate Winslet performing with Weird Al Yankovic. A few favorite songs are "Dog Train," performed by Blues Traveler; "Pots & Pans," by the Bacon Brothers and Mickey Hart; and "(Don't Give Me That) Broccoli," by the Phenomenauts. Boynton illustrates each song with her well-known animals. Lyrics, music, and information about each of the performers are included.

Grandkid Rock, **by Daddy a Go Go (Boyd's Tone Records, 2011).**

Listen to a rock song about superheroes in "I Wanna Be an Action Figure," sports in "The Sports Song," and a remake of "What a Wonderful World."

Greasy Kid Stuff 3: Even More Songs from Inside the Radio **(Confidential Recordings, 2009).**

Two kids' songs are set to punk-rock music: "Spider-Man," by the Mr. T Experience, for those kids who love superheroes, and "Favorite Names," by Key Wilde and Mr. Clarke, which lists a series of most liked names.

"Hip-Hop Humpty Dumpty," from the recording *Banjo to Beatbox*, **by Cathy & Marcy, with Christylez Bacon (Community Music, 2009).**
Introduce children to the concept of beat box and banjo with a hip-hop version of the life and times of Humpty Dumpty.

"I Like Jazz," from the recording *I'm a Rock Star*, **by Joanie Leeds and the Nightlights (Limbostar, 2010).**
Children's songs like "The Alphabet Song," "Twinkle, Twinkle, Little Star," and "Baa, Baa, Black Sheep" are set to a jazz accompaniment. Snap your fingers along with the song.

"It's Time to Get Up," from the recording *It's Time to Get Up! Music for Kids of All Ages!* **by John Bristow (John Bristow and Rockpyle Music, 2011).**
For all the children (and adults!) who don't want to get up in the morning, here's a blues song for you.

Jazz Playground **(Putumayo World Music, 2010).**
Introduce children to jazz from around the world with a variety of performers. Children can stomp, clap, and dance to "Stomp, Stomp," by Lewis Franco and the Missing Cats (United States). Chris McKhool (Canada) sings "Spider-Man." Kinderjazz (Australia) makes up the word *gazooba*. In "Agree and Disagree," by the Mighty Buzzniks (Australia), it's OK to be different because that's what makes us special.

Kid's Country Song and Dance: Action, Sing-Along, Hoe-Down Fun! **by the Learning Station (Monopoli and the Learning Station, 2009).**
Experience a little bit of country with songs like "We've Got Country in Our Body," "Froggy Went A-Courtin'," "Shoo Fly," and "Happy Trails to You." "We've Got Country in Our Body" highlights different instruments you might find in country music, like the cowbell, the harmonica, and the jaw harp. After listening to the first song, have children pay close attention to "Froggy Went A-Courtin'" and see if they can hear which different instruments are being used. Finish the program with the good-bye song "Happy Trails to You."

Kids Meet Composers, **by Wendy Rollin (Wendy Rollin, 2007).**
Introduce children to composers like Bach, Beethoven, Sousa, and Joplin. There's a short piece for each composer that provides biographical information. Then Rollin takes a piece that the composer is known for and creates new lyrics for it.

Ladybug Music: Green Collection, **by Ladybug Music (Ladybug Music, 2011).**
"She'll Be Coming Around the Mountain" has a country twang to the vocals.

Another traditional song, "This Old Man," is a peppy upbeat version with whistles and rhythm sticks.

Ladybug Music: Yellow Collection, by Ladybug Music (Ladybug Music, 2010).

Ladybug Music takes traditional songs and adds different styles of accompaniment. In "Shoo Fly" there is a jazz accompaniment. "Ram Sam Sam" has a groovy rock feel to it.

Let's Go! Travel, Camp and Car Songs, by Susie Tallman and Friends (Rock Me Baby Records, 2007).

For folk songs frequently sung at camp, check out "Polly Wolly Doodle," "Oh! Susanna," and "Home on the Range."

"Like Never Before," from the recording *Oh Lucky Day!* by Lucky Diaz and the Family Jam Band (Rainy Day Dimes Music, 2011).

A pop song encourages children to embrace today and use it to accomplish what they have always wanted to do.

"Little Lamb Jam," from the recording *Wake Up Clarinet!* by Oran Etkin (Oran Etkin's Timbalooloo, 2010).

Listen to a jazz version of the song "Mary Had a Little Lamb."

Make Your Own Someday: Silly Songs for the Shorter Set, by the Jimmies (Pluckypea Records, 2007).

The Jimmies use a variety of musical styles. Rock out with "Cool to Be Uncool," a song about the importance of wearing winter clothes or rain gear even if doing so appears uncool. "Spanimals," a song about the Spanish names of animals, is reminiscent of Carlos Santana's music. A song about covering your mouth when you sneeze, "Do the Elephant," has a pop feel. A down-and-out song about the "Tuesday Blues" of course features the blues. "Huptsha Huptsha" features reggae.

"Molly," from the recording *Rock All Day Rock All Night*, by the Nields (Mercy House Productions, 2008).

The Nields sing a folk song about Molly, a donkey. They spell out the word *Molly*. In each additional verse, they replace a letter with a clap so that by the end they are clapping out the name.

"Oh Susanna," from the recording *Catch the Moon*, by Lisa Loeb and Elizabeth Mitchell (Sheridan Square Records, 2007).

With beautiful vocals and banjo accompaniment, Loeb and Mitchell record a traditional version of "Oh Susanna." For another version, check out "Oh Susanna" performed by Rhythm Child on the recording *Rock & Roll Playground* (Putumayo World Music, 2010).

Piano Music for Children **(Dal Segno, 2009).**

Selections of classical music have been chosen for children. Some of the pieces include "Russian Dance," from the Nutcracker Suite, by Peter Tchaikovsky; "The Swan," from Camille Saint-Saëns's *Carnival of the Animals*; and "Kickin' the Clouds Away," by George Gershwin. If you're looking for classical music to play in the background, this is a good CD, because it has a variety of pieces with different moods, some quiet and restful, and others energetic and enthusiastic.

"Pickle in the Middle Blues," from the recording *Pickle in the Middle Blues*, by Kim Weitkamp (Kim Weitkamp, 2010).

While Weitkamp shares her thoughts about being a middle child, her band plays blues music in the background. This would also be a good piece to use to introduce the harmonica.

You'll Sing a Song and I'll Sing a Song, **by Ella Jenkins (Smithsonian/Folkways Records, 1989).**

Jenkins includes a couple of versions of two folk songs, "You'll Sing a Song and I'll Sing a Song" and "Miss Mary Mack" or "May-ree Mack."

CHAPTER 9
ANIMAL ANTICS

To get children thinking about the theme of this program, ask them to name animals that make music. Birds will probably come to mind first, but ask them if other animals make music, too. Have them think about their favorite animals and the sounds they make. Is their dog's howling music? What about the sounds of crickets and bullfrogs in the summer?

A few instruments look and sound like animals. Guiros are ridged percussion instruments. Musicians run a stick over the ridges to make music. Some guiros are designed to look like animals. The most common animal shape is a frog, which comes in a variety of sizes, but some companies also create guiros in the shape of turtles, crocodiles, and snails. The frogs are great to use in a program, because when you run the wooden dowel over the ridges, it sounds like the "ribbit" of a frog. Ocarinas are instruments that make animal sounds. Sometimes they look like birds, and they chirp or whistle when you blow into them. These instruments are usually inexpensive and can be ordered online.

The program playlist features several different animals, but there are enough resources listed in the bonus sections for a more focused theme on dogs, zoo animals, farm animals, or animal habitats.

PROGRAM PLAYLIST

▶ Opening Song: "Bear to the Left," from the recording *Ranky Tanky*, by Rani Arbo and Daisy Mayhem
▶ Book: *I Got Two Dogs*, by John Lithgow and illustrated by Robert Neubecker

- ▶ Song: "My Dog Rags," from the recording *Hot Peas 'n Butter*, vol. 2, *A Second Helping*, by Hot Peas 'n Butter
- ▶ Book: *Me and My Animal Friends*, by Ralph Covert and illustrated by Laurie Keller
- ▶ Song: "Tiny Tim," from the recording *Ladybug Music: Yellow Collection*, by Ladybug Music
- ▶ Book: *A Crazy Day at the Critter Café*, by Barbara Odanaka and illustrated by Lee White
- ▶ Song: "Animal Adventure," from the recording *The Animal Faire*, by Tony Robinson
- ▶ Book: *There Was an Old Lady Who Swallowed Some Bugs*, adapted and illustrated by Johnette Downing
- ▶ Activity: "Doggie, Doggie, Who Has the Bone?" from *Wee Sing Games, Games, Games*, by Pamela Conn Beall and Susan Hagen Nipp and illustrated by Nancy Spence Klein
- ▶ Musical instrument: Jingle-Bell Wristlet

Opening Song

"Bear to the Left," from the recording *Ranky Tanky*, by Rani Arbo and Daisy Mayhem (Mayhem Music, 2010).

In this action song, movements are described by the names of animals, like *bear* or *snake*. The names can also be used as verbs.

Book

***I Got Two Dogs*, by John Lithgow and illustrated by Robert Neubecker (Simon & Schuster Books for Young Readers, 2008).**

The book comes with a CD of Lithgow singing an ode to two dogs Fanny and Blue; one is twelve and the other is two. They're the best dogs in the world even though they don't know tricks and chew shoes. Throughout the song there are words with extended o vowels that can be howled like a dog. Encourage children to sing along.

Song

"My Dog Rags," from the recording *Hot Peas 'n Butter*, vol. 2, *A Second Helping*, by Hot Peas 'n Butter (Hot Peas 'n Butter, 2010).
The dog Rags has his own dance style. Join in with the motions.

Book

Me and My Animal Friends, by Ralph Covert and illustrated by Laurie Keller (Henry Holt, 2009).
A boy and girl beg their parents for a pet and imagine all the options in the world from antelopes and penguins to ocelots and sloths. So many wonderful choices! If you want to sing the story, lyrics and chords are included at the end of the book, or you can visit the website (http://us.macmillan.com/meandmyanimalfriends/RalphCovert) to watch a clip of Covert performing the song. After sharing the story, read "A Note from Ralph," and ask children what type of pet they would like if they could pick anything they wanted.

Song

"Tiny Tim," from the recording *Ladybug Music: Yellow Collection*, by Ladybug Music (Ladybug Music, 2010).
There are a lot of versions of this song, including some that are used for hand clapping and jumping rope. This version has a 1950s rock feel. Clap along to the rhythm.

Book

A Crazy Day at the Critter Café, by Barbara Odanaka and illustrated by Lee White (Margaret K. McElderry Books, 2009).
A bus breaks down outside of the Critter Café, and all sorts of animals (including an elephant band) stream into the restaurant. It's a chaotic mess, with animals like raccoons, macaws, rams, and penguins asking for or complaining about their food. On top of all the whirlwind and craziness, there's a skateboarding cow. Will the waiter and cook be able to successfully feed this difficult crowd? The rhyming text and illustrations make this story laugh-out-loud funny.

Song

"Animal Adventure," from the recording *The Animal Faire*, by Tony Robinson (Tony Robinson Music, 2011).

Listen to the different animal and nature sounds as they combine to create a night song. See if participants can guess which animals are making each noise. Pass out paper and pencil and have them write down what they hear as they listen to the song. Each song on the recording is performed as if by an animal. For example, the Dingos sing "Dirty Dog Day," and Mari Posa performs "Fly with Me" featuring Dr. Monkey.

Book

***There Was an Old Lady Who Swallowed Some Bugs*, adapted and illustrated by Johnette Downing (Pelican Publishing, 2010).**

An old lady swallows a spider, a flea, an ant, a cockroach, and more. The story concludes with a surprise ending. Downing performs this song on her album *Boogie Woogie Bugs* (Wiggle Worm Records, 2010). You can share the book by singing or chanting the song yourself or by playing her recording. The collage illustrations lend themselves to being adapted into a flannel story.

Activity

"Doggie, Doggie, Who Has the Bone?"

In this game, someone is chosen to be the doggy and someone else has stolen the "bone." The person who is the doggy has to figure out who in the group has the bone. This is one of many great games and songs from *Wee Sing Games, Games, Games*, by Pamela Conn Beall and Susan Hagen Nipp and illustrated by Nancy Spence Klein (Price Stern Sloan, 2002). Packaged with a CD, the book has a large variety of games, many of which are musical and some of which feature animals. If you want to add games or movement activities to programs, this is a great resource.

Musical Instrument
Jingle-Bell Wristlets

Supplies:

- ▶ Pipe cleaners: 1 per child
- ▶ Jingle bells: 2 or 3 per child (make sure the jingle bells are large enough so that the pipe cleaner fits through the top of the bell).
- ▶ Tape

Directions:

- ▶ Have children thread one jingle bell on to the pipe cleaner. Twist the pipe cleaner around the bell to keep it in place.
- ▶ Thread the other jingle bells on to the pipe cleaner in the same manner.
- ▶ Connect the two ends of the pipe cleaner to form a circle, and tape the spot where the ends meet so the wire ends don't stick through and scratch people.
- ▶ Children can wear the jingle bell wristlet like a bracelet or hold on to it like a tambourine and shake it while listening to the song "Tiny Tim."

BONUS BOOKS

Bad Boys Get Henpecked! by Margie Palatini and illustrated by Henry Cole (Katherine Tegen Books, 2009).
Wolves Willy and Wally crave chicken. They work out a devious plan to dress up like chickens and pretend they are the Handy-Dandy Lupino Brothers, thereby tricking Mrs. Hen into letting them come into the hen house. Mrs. Hen, excited for the help, gives the boys a long list of chores. While one works his way through the chores, the other watches the many baby chicks. After a bit they are too tired to do anything but take a nap, leaving the chicks to their own devices. When Mrs. Hen walks in, the two Bad Boys are in big trouble! For more adventures with Willy and Wally, check out *Bad Boys* (Katherine Tegen Books, 2003) and *Bad Boys Get Cookie!* (Katherine Tegen Books, 2006).

The Carnival of the Animals, **with music by Camille Saint-Saëns, new verses by Jack Prelutsky, and illustrated by Mary GrandPré (Alfred A. Knopf, 2010).**
In 1886 Camille Saint-Saëns created *The Carnival of the Animals,* a compilation of musical vignettes, each one featuring a different animal like the lion, the rooster, and the tortoise. Prelutsky has added poems to go along with the pieces. An accompanying CD features Prelutsky reading his poetry before the musical selections. Like Sergei Prokofiev's *Peter and the Wolf,* Saint-Saëns's work is an engaging way to introduce children to classical music. Share a few of the selections with children, and have them listen to the music and act as that animal would act, or play the CD in the background while children work on an activity.

Chicken Dance, **by Tammi Sauer and illustrated by Dan Santat (Sterling, 2009).**
Marge and Lola, two chickens, vow to win the local Barnyard Talent Show because the grand prize is a ticket to see their favorite singer, Elvis Poultry. The animals that stand between them and winning are the ducks. Before the chickens can compete, they need to figure out their talent. Can they find something special to do in time for the talent show, or will the ducks win again?

The Croaky Pokey! **by Ethan Long (Holiday House, 2011).**
A group of frogs dance to their own version of the "Hokey Pokey" while another group plays their musical instruments. As they are dancing, they try to catch flies, but with little luck. Read the book once through and then repeat the story while children act out the different verses.

Don't Wake Mr. Bear! **by Jill Newton (Egmont, 2011).**
Winter is coming, and it's time for Dormouse and others to hibernate. Dormouse brings together the woodland orchestra, and they each play their soothing instruments: flutes, xylophones, and harps. The gentle music makes Dormouse sleepy. Before he goes to bed, he admonishes the animals that they mustn't wake Bear. Unfortunately, the wolves didn't get the message, and when they decide it's time for a musical party with horns and drums, Bear wakes up much too early. Find out why it's not good to wake up animals when they are hibernating.

Hans My Hedgehog: A Tale from the Brothers Grimm, **by Kate Coombs and illustrated by John Nickle (Atheneum Books for Young Readers, 2012).**
In a gentler version of a Brothers Grimm fairy tale, a couple wishes for a baby but instead gets Hans the Hedgehog, part boy and part animal. It's a story of a curse, a spoiled princess, a musical hedgehog, and a happily every after. Despite the beautiful music he can play on his fiddle, no one

wants to be friends with Hans. He leaves with his herd of pigs for the forest. When a king is lost in the forest, Hans helps him for a promise: to send Hans the person who greets the king upon his return home. Although the king makes the promise, he chooses not to fulfill it when that person is his daughter. Later, another king is lost, and Hans presents the same deal. Will this king keep his promise, and will Hans finally leave the forest?

If You're Hoppy, by April Pulley Sayre and illustrated by Jackie Urbanovic (Greenwillow Books, 2011).

Sayre uses the traditional song "If You're Happy and You Know It" to talk about animals with similar characteristics. For example, the first verse mentions animals that are "hoppy," including rabbits, frogs, and crickets. The next verse focuses on animals that are "sloppy." Extend the story by asking children to brainstorm more animals that fall in those categories, or ask children to create new verses, like "If you're lazy and you know it, you're a sloth."

Jo MacDonald Saw a Pond, by Mary Quattlebaum and illustrated by Laura J. Bryant (Dawn Publications, 2011).

Old MacDonald's granddaughter Jo takes a nature walk and encounters various animals like deer, ducks, and frogs milling around the pond. In this new version of "Old MacDonald," each verse introduces an animal or nature object and its accompanying sound. At the end of the book children can test their memory by matching the picture of an animal or nature object with its corresponding sound. Additional facts are included about pond ecosystems and the animals mentioned. There are also suggested activities that children can do to experience nature. Jo uses a notebook to record what she observes. A follow-up activity could be to have children create and decorate their own nature notebook.

Man Gave Names to All the Animals, by Bob Dylan illustrated by Jim Arnosky (Sterling 2010).

Bob Dylan's song "Man Gave Names to All the Animals" is about naming different animals and is accompanied by beautifully detailed illustrations by Jim Arnosky. Teach children the chorus, and they can join in as you play the CD. Afterward, children can pour over the book and try to find the more than 170 animals that are in the illustrations!

A Pig Parade Is a Terrible Idea, by Michael Ian Black and illustrated by Kevin Hawkes (Simon & Schuster Books for Young Readers, 2010).

A pig parade sounds like it would be a great idea, right? Wrong! Pigs are terrible parade participants, because they don't march. They don't like floats (except for root-beer floats!), and they have hooves, which make balloon handling very difficult. Before sharing the story, brainstorm with children why they think a pig parade wouldn't work. Make a list of pig traits. Then share the story and see what they get right.

The Rainforest Grew All Around, by Susan K. Mitchell and illustrated by Connie McLennan (Sylvan Dell Publishing, 2007).

Learn about the rain-forest ecosystem by singing this song to the tune of the folk song "The Green Grass Grew All Around." Each verse highlights an animal or object from nature. Make the story interactive by providing children with a picture of the animal or nature object mentioned at the beginning of each verse. Attach a piece of mural paper to the wall, or use a whiteboard and write "Rain Forest" at the top. Then when the children hear their word, have them attach the piece of paper to the mural. If you have many participants, multiple children can have pictures of the same animal or object. At the end of the story, you will have a rain-forest mural. After sharing the book, talk about the additional factual information that is highlighted in the panels on each two-page spread. The author also includes two activities to help children understand what kind of adaptations animals and plants have so that they can inhabit the rain forest. She finishes the book with a recipe for "Rainforest Cookies." Included are questions to help children think about what types of food items come from the rain forest.

Ten on the Sled, by Kim Norman and illustrated by Liza Woodruff (Sterling, 2010).

Ten Arctic animals, including a wolf, a hare, and a walrus, take a toboggan ride. As they slide down a hill, one animal after another falls off the sled and is enveloped in a rolling snowball that keeps pace with the sledding animals. Sing this song to the tune "Ten in the Bed."

There Was an Old Monkey Who Swallowed a Frog, by Jennifer Ward and illustrated by Steve Gray (Marshall Cavendish Children, 2010).

A silly monkey swallows all manner of rain-forest animals and nature in this comical adaptation of "There Was an Old Lady Who Swallowed a Fly." Each of the characters has dramatic facial expressions that add to the humor. Some of the items swallowed include a cocoa bean, a cat, and a tapir. For a Southwestern desert version of this story, check out *There Was a Coyote Who Swallowed a Flea* (Rising Moon, 2007). Coyote swallows a rattler, a chili, a cactus, and cowboy attire.

Way Up in the Arctic, by Jennifer Ward and illustrated by Kenneth J. Spengler (Rising Moon, 2007).

In an Arctic version of the rhyme "Over in the Meadow," caribou, polar bears, walruses, and more interact with their habitat. The illustrations, as well as three pages of additional facts, help children understand the Arctic habitat. Each two-page spread has a number hidden in the illustrations. A musical score is included. If you like this story, check out the author's two other books based on the same rhyme: *Somewhere in the Ocean* (Rising Moon, 2000) and *Over in the Garden* (Rising Moon, 2002).

What Animals Really Like, by Fiona Robinson (Abrams Books for Young Readers, 2011).

A maestro introduces a new piece to the audience about animals and what they enjoy doing. The animals start singing a nice rhyming song, and all is going well, until they begin to deviate from the original composition. It seems they don't really like the stereotypical things the maestro has mentioned. Instead, they like to play ping-pong and blow bubbles and do other things the maestro doesn't know about. They want to perform the song but with newer, truer lyrics.

What's New at the Zoo? by Betty Comden and Adolph Green and illustrated by Travis Foster (Blue Apple Books, 2011).

Read the picture-book version of the song "What's New at the Zoo?" taken from the 1960 Broadway musical *Do Re Mi*. In the song, animals want out of the zoo because it is overpopulated and they are stepping all over one another. The illustrations are energetic, with bold typeface for when the animals speak. Pair this with a recording of the song. One version can be found on the recording *Do Re Mi: The Original London Cast* (Sepia Records Limited, 2011).

BONUS TRACKS

Boogie Woogie Bugs, by Johnette Downing (Wiggle Worm Records, 2010).

Downing, a musician from Louisiana, has many entertaining songs about bugs on this recording. Learn about the anatomy of an insect by singing "Head Thorax Abdomen" to the tune "Head, Shoulders, Knees, and Toes." The bluesy song "Cockroach" describes the lonely life of a disliked bug who just wants to be loved. "Sly Slug" is a tongue twister sung to the tune "The Battle Hymn of the Republic." Try to sing along as the tempo increases.

"Bunny Hop," from the recording *The Hollow Trees*, by the Hollow Trees (Water Music Records, 2008).

Hop like a bunny and make the sounds of an assortment of animals.

"Free Little Bird," from the recording *Catch the Moon*, by Lisa Loeb and Elizabeth Mitchell (Sheridan Square Records, 2007).

This gentle song combines two traditional folk songs, "Free Little Bird" and "Mole in the Ground." Another option for "Mole in the Ground" is found on the recording *Birds, Beasts, Bugs and Fishes (Little and Big)*, by Pete Seeger (Smithsonian Folkways Recordings, 1998).

"Good Dog Time," from the recording *If I Were a Dog*, by Robbie Long (Sumner Music, 2011).

What would cause a dog to have a fun time? Ask children what they think dogs like to do.

I Heart Earth, by Lucas Miller (Bio Rhythms, 2011).

Miller features different songs about animals, including "I'm a Mako Shark," which talks about the food chain; "The Anaconda La Bamba," about a large snake; and "Stinkle, Stinkle, Little Skunky," a lullaby about skunks sung to the tune of "Twinkle, Twinkle, Little Star."

"My Flea Has Dogs," from the recording *Sing Along!*, by Caspar Babypants (Aurora Elephant Music, 2011).

In this twist, a dog doesn't have fleas. It's the reverse. The song mentions many dog breeds.

"Peep Squirrel," from the recording *Ladybug Music: Green Collection*, by Ladybug Music (Ladybug Music, 2011).

While listening to this song, pretend to be a squirrel and do the actions described.

Pickle in the Middle Blues, by Kim Weitkamp (Kim Weitkamp, 2010).

In "Work Then Play," Weitkamp tells a story about a lazy grasshopper, an eager and hardworking ant, and the lesson that the lazy grasshopper learns. For another story about an ant and a grasshopper, try *Ant and Grasshopper*, by Luli Gray and illustrated by Giuliano Ferri (Margaret K. McElderry Books, 2011). Weitkamp also sings a song about the joy of finding ants and anthills in the rock anthem "The Anthill Song."

"Talk to the Animals," from the recording *Radio Wayne*, by Wayne Brady (Walt Disney Records, 2011).

Brady envisions what it might be like if people could communicate with animals. The song has animal sounds in the background.

***There's a Train . . .*, by We Kids Rock! (We Kids Rock, 2009).**
Rock along with the silly rhyming song "Down by the Bay" that mentions animals. It's time to go fishing with the traditional song "Crawdad."

"Weirder Than Weird Animals," from the recording *Imagination Generation*, by David Kisor (Growing Sound, 2010).
Combine three animal names into one to create an unusual animal concoction. Afterward, encourage children to pick three animal names and combine them into a new animal. Then have them draw the animal and describe what it likes to eat, where it lives, and other animal traits.

"Wimoweh (The Lion Sleeps Tonight)," from the recording *For Kids and Just Plain Folks*, by Pete Seeger (Sony Music Entertainment, 1997).
Seeger performs his own version in front of a live audience. It's not the whole song, but it's the part everyone loves to sing. For another version, listen to Ladysmith Black Mambazo, on *Love and Peace: Greatest Hits for Kids* (Music for Little People, 2010). In the beginning of the song, the singer sets the scene. A family is in the jungle, and a young boy hears all of the wild animals and is afraid. The song is a lullaby that his family sings to calm his fears.

CHAPTER 10
CAMP DO RE MI

hether it's sleeping in a tent in the backyard or hiking in the woods at nature camp, there are always stories to tell, songs to sing, and adventures to be had. To open the program, ask children whether they have been camping before and what they remember best about their camping experiences. Then say, "We're going to have our own little camping trip at Camp [insert library name]. First we have to pack for our trip." Hold up a backpack with some things you would need for camping (such as sunblock, a can of baked beans, a flashlight) and some things you shouldn't bring (a hair dryer, TV remote, a fast-food wrapper), and ask them if they would need this item or that item. Finish by holding up a book and CD, and talk about how fun it is when camping to tell stories and sing camp songs.

PROGRAM PLAYLIST

- ▶ Opening Song: "The Wake Up Song," from the recording *Camp Lisa*, by Lisa Loeb
- ▶ Book: *Froggy Goes to Camp*, by Jonathan London and illustrated by Frank Remkiewicz
- ▶ Book: *Mosquitoes Are Ruining My Summer! and Other Silly Dilly Camp Songs*, by Alan Katz and illustrated by David Catrow
- ▶ Song: "Madalina Catalina," from the recording *Let's Go! Travel, Camp and Car Songs*, by Susie Tallman and Friends
- ▶ Book: *Tacky Goes to Camp*, by Helen Lester and illustrated by Lynn Munsinger
- ▶ Song: "Black Socks," from the recording *Scat Like That: a Musical Word Odyssey*, by Cathy Fink and Marcy Marxer

- ▶ Book: *Scare a Bear*, by Kathy-jo Wargin and illustrated by John Bendall-Brunello
- ▶ Activity: "L-I-M-B-O," from *Mosquitoes Are Ruining My Summer! and Other Silly Dilly Camp Songs*, by Alan Katz and illustrated by David Catrow
- ▶ Musical Instrument: Kazoo

Opening Song

"The Wake Up Song," from the recording *Camp Lisa*, by Lisa Loeb (Furious Rose Productions, 2008).
Wake up to the bugle call and join in the fun by clapping and stomping to the rhythm of the song.

Book

Froggy Goes to Camp, by Jonathan London and illustrated by Frank Remkiewicz (Viking, 2008).
Froggy is super excited to attend Camp Run-a-Muck until he gets there and doesn't know anyone but the camp director, his principal Mr. Mugwort. As he acclimates to camp, Froggy enjoys experiences with archery and swimming, but his klutzy moves often have disastrous and funny results with Mr. Mugwort. The story includes two songs that the campers sing: "Dear Mama Duck, Dear Papa Duck," based on the song "Hello Muddah, Hello Fadduh," and "Beans, Beans, the Musical Fruit."

Book

Mosquitoes Are Ruining My Summer! and Other Silly Dilly Camp Songs, by Alan Katz and illustrated by David Catrow (Margaret K. McElderry Books, 2011).
Author Alan Katz and illustrator David Catrow are at it again with a humorous collection of camp songs set to familiar tunes. Try "Somebody Send Me Home Now!" an ode to awful camp food sung to the tune of "Skip to My Lou." Also, "The Laundry Blues," sung to the tune of "The Mexican Hat Dance," will have children giggling about smelly camp clothes.

Song

"Madalina Catalina," from the recording *Let's Go! Travel, Camp and Car Songs*, by Susie Tallman and Friends (Rock Me Baby Records, 2007).

For this song, have a poster with Madalina's long name spelled out and use the poster to help teach children Madalina's full name. After practicing a few times slowly and than faster and faster, try it with the music. Part of the fun is the silliness of the name, but part of it is that the song is so fast, it's hard to say her whole name without getting tongue-tied.

Book

Tacky Goes to Camp, by Helen Lester and illustrated by Lynn Munsinger (Houghton Mifflin Books for Children, 2009).

Goodly, Lovely, Angel, Neatly, Perfect, and Tacky are going to Camp Whoopihaha. All the other campers bring camping supplies like a flashlight, a first-aid kit, and a backpack, but Tacky brings cookies, roller skates, and a TV. One night all the penguins tell scary stories around the campfire. When it's Tacky's turn, his story about a bear named Beware ends up not being scary at all. While he is sleeping though, his story becomes real when an actual bear visits the camp looking for food. Can Tacky save the day? The penguins sing a song around the campfire that you can also teach to children.

Song

"Black Socks," from the recording *Scat Like That: a Musical Word Odyssey*, by Cathy Fink and Marcy Marxer (Rounder Records, 2005).

Join in this fun song about socks that get better with age. Once the children learn how to sing the song, try performing it in a round.

Book

Scare a Bear, by Kathy-jo Wargin and illustrated by John Bendall-Brunello (Sleeping Bear Press, 2010).

Fellow campers brainstorm about what can scare a bear. What if creating a noise, dousing it with water, or making a scary face won't work? What should the campers do next?

Activity

Share the song "L-I-M-B-O" from *Mosquitoes Are Ruining My Summer! and Other Silly Dilly Camp Songs*, by Alan Katz and illustrated by David Catrow (Margaret K. McElderry Books, 2011). Have children sing the song to the tune of "B-I-N-G-O," and then play a game of limbo.

Musical Instrument
Kazoo

Supplies:
- ▶ Paper-towel tubes or gift-wrap tubes cut into 5-inch lengths: 1 per child
- ▶ Wax paper cut into 4-inch-by-4-inch squares: 1 piece per child
- ▶ Masking or duct tape
- ▶ Decorating materials

Directions:
- ▶ Before the program, cut the paper-towel tubes or gift-wrap tubes into 5-inch pieces.
- ▶ Have children attach a square of wax paper to one end of the tube with tape.
- ▶ Decorate the tube with stickers, markers, or crayons.
- ▶ Hum into the open end to create the kazoo sound.
- ▶ Play the song "Black Socks," and have children hum along with their kazoos.

BONUS BOOKS

Buster Goes to Cowboy Camp, **by Denise Fleming (Henry Holt and Company, 2008).**
Brown Shoes leaves on vacation, and Buster, the pet dog, has to go to Sagebrush Kennels for Cowboy Camp. Unsure about the camp, it takes some time for Buster to get over his homesickness. After trying out art projects, buckaroo ball, and cowboy songs, Buster thinks he just might be enjoying cowboy camp after all.

A Couple of Boys Have the Best Week Ever, **by Marla Frazee (Harcourt, 2008).**
James and Eamon have the best week ever when they stay at Eamon's grandparents' home and attend nature camp. Although nature camp isn't exactly thrilling, the boys create their own fun by playing together and with Eamon's grandparents.

Duck Tents, **by Lynne Berry and illustrated by Hiroe Nakata (Henry Holt and Company, 2009).**
Five little ducks go camping. They fish and roast marshmallows and go to sleep in their own tent. That's when they hear a spooky sound and have to find a way to soothe their fears.

The Jellybeans and the Big Camp Kickoff, **by Laura Numeroff and Nate Evans and illustrated by Lynn Munsinger (Abrams Books for Young Readers, 2011).**
Emily, Bitsy, Anna, and Nicole are friends attending camp. Each has her own talent and enjoyable activity at camp. Emily dances, Bitsy creates arts and crafts, and Anna explores books about nature. Nicole lives for soccer, but the camp has gymnastics, kayaking, and tennis—no soccer. Can Nicole's friends help her find something exciting to do at camp?

Ricky Is Brave, **by Guido Van Genechten (Clavis, 2011).**
In this story about overcoming fear, Ricky decides he is old enough and brave enough to sleep outside by himself in a tent. At first it seems to be a night of adventure, but when Ricky hears spooky sounds and sees scary shadows, he isn't so sure about staying outside alone.

BONUS TRACKS

"Boom, Boom, Ain't It Great to Be Crazy," from the recording *Ladybug Music: Green Collection,* **by Ladybug Music (Ladybug Music, 2011).**
Children can join in the catchy chorus of this silly camp song.

Camp Lisa, **by Lisa Loeb (Furious Rose Productions, 2008).**
"Father Abraham" and "Peanut Butter & Jelly" are great action songs to use with children. Tongue twisters are another fun camp activity. Loeb records several "Woodchuck" tracks to help children learn the tongue twister.

"A Day at Camp Decibel," from the recording *Making Good Noise,* **by Tom Chapin (Sundance Music, 2003).**
Ten bugle calls are combined to create the song. Use the song as background music before the program starts and for the limbo game. The song spans a day at camp and all the funny and crazy things that happen.

"Hello Muddah, Hello Faddah," from the recording *Grandkid Rock*, by Daddy a Go Go (Boyd's Tone Records, 2011).

Clap along to a song about overcoming homesickness at camp.

"I Love Camping," from the recording *We Are the Not Its!* by the Not Its! (Little Loopy Records, 2009).

The Not Its! sing about hiking, canoeing, mosquitoes, and the joy of camping.

Let's Go! Travel, Camp and Car Songs, by Susie Tallman and Friends (Rock Me Baby Records, 2007).

In addition to the two songs listed already, this CD has many traditional camping songs like "Going on a Bear Hunt," "A Sailor Went to Sea," and "The Ostrich Song."

"Poison Ivy," from the recording *Jim Gill Sings the Sneezing Song and Other Contagious Tunes*, by Jim Gill (Jim Gill Music, 1993).

What's a camp theme without a reference to poison ivy? Learn about poison ivy and where it can be found while singing this entertaining song about the evil plant and the scratching that ensues.

CHAPTER 11
DRAGONS, MONSTERS, AND GHOSTS, OH MY!

se the books and songs in this chapter to create a slightly scary, very silly event featuring dragons, ghosts, monsters, witches, werewolves, mummies, and other creepy creatures. Although some books and songs in the bonus sections mention Halloween, most do not.

To introduce the theme, ask children about their favorite monsters and the noises they make. If you have musical instruments like shakers, rhythm sticks, or other percussion instruments, this is a great theme to use to introduce them. Several of the stories listed below can be enhanced with musical instruments.

PROGRAM PLAYLIST

▶ Opening Song: "Monster Mash," by Andrew Gold and Linda Ronstadt, from the recording *Love and Peace: Greatest Hits for Kids*

▶ Book: *Over in the Hollow*, by Rebecca Dickinson and illustrated by Stephan Britt

▶ Book: *Bedtime at the Swamp*, by Kristyn Crow and illustrated by Macky Pamintuan

▶ Song: "Monster Boogie," from the recording *The Best of the Laurie Berkner Band*, by the Laurie Berkner Band

▶ Book: *If You're a Monster and You Know It*, by Rebecca Emberley and illustrated by Ed Emberley

▶ Song: "Dry Bones," from the recording *Wee Sing for Halloween*, by Pamela Conn Beall and Susan Hagen Nipp

- ▶ Book: *Frankie Stein*, by Lola M. Schaefer and illustrated by Kevan Atteberry
- ▶ Activity: Monster Puppets
- ▶ Musical Instrument: Monster Shakers

Opening Song

"Monster Mash," by Andrew Gold and Linda Ronstadt, from the recording *Love and Peace: Greatest Hits for Kids* (Music for Little People, 2010). Teach children how to do some 1960s dance moves like the twist and the mashed potato, but have them do the moves as if they are a monster or a zombie.

Book

Over in the Hollow, by Rebecca Dickinson and illustrated by Stephan Britt (Chronicle Books, 2009). A spooky hollow teems with thirteen types of creepy creatures, including vampires, ghosts, spiders, mummies, owls, and skeletons. A new take on the poem "Over in the Meadow," by Olive A. Wadsworth, you can teach children to act out some of the verses.

Book

Bedtime at the Swamp, by Kristyn Crow and illustrated by Macky Pamintuan (HarperCollins, 2008). It's nighttime, and a boy is sitting in the swamp humming a song when he says:

> "I heard . . .
> Splish splash
> rumba-rumba
> bim bam BOOM!
> Splish splash
> rumba-rumba
> bim bam BOOM!"[1]

He fears that a monster is in the swamp with him and runs and hides. His sister finds him in a tree and says that it is time for bed. He replies that there is a monster in the swamp. When she hears the same sounds, she hides, too. The story repeats with various family members coming to tell them that it is time for bed and then hiding when they hear the rhythmic noise of someone or something stomping through the forest. Is a monster really out to get them? When you read this book, you can sing the refrain to a simple tune that you create or chant it. It's also great for rhythm sticks. Have children tap their rhythm sticks on the ground (tap) and then hit their rhythm sticks together (clap). As you are chanting the refrain, they do the following rhythm pattern twice: tap, tap, clap, clap, tap, clap, tap.

Song

"Monster Boogie," from the recording *The Best of the Laurie Berkner Band*, by the Laurie Berkner Band (Two Tomatoes Records, 2010).
Invite children to dance like a monster.

Book

If You're a Monster and You Know It, by Rebecca Emberley and illustrated by Ed Emberley (Orchard Books, 2010).
On the basis of the song "If You're Happy and You Know It," the Emberleys have created a new monster version. Visit Scholastic's website (www.scholastic.com/ifyoureamonsterandyouknowit) to listen to Adrian Emberley perform the song. Adrian uses musical instruments to help illustrate the monster noises. If you have a variety of instruments, pass them around to the children. Discuss the different verses, and ask them what instrument they think should be used for each one. Then share the book twice, singing the song and having the children join in with their instrument when it is their turn.

Song

"Dry Bones," from the recording *Wee Sing for Halloween*, by Pamela Conn Beall and Susan Hagen Nipp (Price Stern Sloan, 2006).
The book comes with a CD of spooky music, rhymes, stories, and even a game. "Dry Bones" is an adapted version of the traditional spiritual song. Children can point to the different body parts as they are mentioned in the song. Also included on the CD are songs like "Spooky Loo," sung to the tune of "Here We Go Looby Loo"; "The Ghosts Go Flying," sung to the tune "The Ants Go Marching"; and the traditional ghostly song "Skin and Bones."

Book

Frankie Stein, **by Lola M. Schaefer and illustrated by Kevan Atteberry (Marshall Cavendish Children, 2007).**

Frankie Stein, born to monster parents, looks nothing like them—no warts, no rotten teeth, no scary blue hair. Instead, he appears to be a normal human baby. The horror! His parents give him lessons in scaring others, but Frankie doesn't seem to have the knack. In the end, though, he develops his own way to scare his parents. The humorous twist will have the audience laughing.

Activity
Monster Puppets

Clean out your craft closet and fill a table with leftover felt, construction paper, pom-poms, ribbon, and buttons. Give children a brown-paper lunch bag, and encourage them to design their own monster puppet. The folded bottom of the bag is the face. Children can make their puppets as crazy or creepy or silly as they want.

Musical Instrument
Monster Shakers

Supplies:

- ▶ Monster puppets children have made in the previous activity
- ▶ Dried beans
- ▶ Yarn or tape
- ▶ Newspaper

Directions:

- ▶ Once children are done making their monster puppet, have them fill the paper bag with dried beans and crumbled newspaper.
- ▶ Tie the end of the bag shut with yarn or close it with tape.
- ▶ The gathered end is the handle.
- ▶ Shake your monster to Laurie Berkner's song "Monster Boogie."

BONUS BOOKS

Bone Soup, by Cambria Evans (Houghton Mifflin Company, 2008).

Ever-hungry Finnigin searches for a Halloween feast. When the "towns-creatures" hear of Finnigin the Eater, they hide their containers of eye-balls, bat wings, and frog legs. No one shares food with Finnigin, so he decides to make bone soup. He lures the creatures out with his song "Bone Soup." Similar to the traditional tale "Stone Soup," Finnigin tells the town's creatures that the soup would be tastier with additional ingredients, and the creatures are so enthralled with the idea of the magical soup that they bring their delicacies like toenail clippings and dried mouse droppings. The whole town joins in the Halloween feast.

Boy Dumplings, by Ying Chang Compestine and illustrated by James Yamasaki (Holiday House, 2009).

In this clever story a young boy outsmarts the ghost who kidnapped him. A boy uses the light from his lantern to scare off ghosts, but when his lantern goes out, a ghost snatches him. Before the ghost eats the boy for dinner, the boy tells him he has a perfect recipe for boy dumplings. The ghost thinks that boy dumplings sound wonderfully delightful, so he scurries around all night long finding garlic, onions, cabbage, soy sauce, and an extremely large steamer. He's so preoccupied gathering the ingredients that he doesn't realize the boy's devious plan until it's too late.

Dragons and Monsters, by Matthew Reinhart and Robert Sabuda (Candlewick Press, 2011).

Where do people think the yeti lives? What does a kraken look like? What's the difference between a gold dragon and a black dragon? Children who love reading about mythical creatures will enjoy finding the answers to those questions in this pop-up book.

Hush, Baby Ghostling, by Andrea Beaty and illustrated by Pascal Lemaitre (Margaret K. McElderry Books, 2009).

What are ghosts afraid of? A new take on the traditional song "Hush Little Baby," this soothing lullaby encourages Baby Ghostling to leave his worries behind and instead dream of monsters, ghouls, owls, and banshees.

Hush, Little Dragon, by Boni Ashburn and illustrated by Kelly Murphy (Abrams Books for Young Readers, 2008).

In this version of "Hush, Little Baby" a mother dragon sings to her young-ster, promising gifts of a princess, knights, three musketeers, a magician, and more.

I Want My Light On! **by Tony Ross (Andersen Press, 2010).**

Little Princess won't go to sleep without her light on because she is sure a ghost hides under her bed. The king, the admiral, the doctor, and the maid all assure her that there are no ghosts. A twist at the end shows that she's not the only one who wants her light on.

One Drowsy Dragon, **by Ethan Long (Orchard Books, 2010).**

One drowsy dragon tries to sleep but can't because of all the noise his siblings are making, from tapping during dance lessons to wrestling with each other to shrieking while watching TV. The noise makes the dragon more and more mad. When everyone finally tries to sleep, something surprising makes the most noise.

Over at the Castle, **by Boni Ashburn and illustrated by Kelly Murphy (Abrams Books for Young Readers, 2010).**

Ashburn's medieval version of "Over in the Meadow" features one baby dragon, two guards, three little lords, four servants, and so on. Throughout the day, castle workers keep busy weaving, cleaning, and cooking, and the guards and knights keep watch to see what the dragons will do. What are the mama and baby dragon waiting for?

Sipping Spiders through a Straw: Campfire Songs for Monsters, **by Kelly DiPucchio and illustrated by Gris Grimly (Scholastic Press, 2008).**

This book uses traditional songs like "Take Me Out to the Ball Game" and "Home on the Range" and turns them into songs that monsters will enjoy. For instance, those songs are adapted to "Take Me Out to the Graveyard" and "Home of the Strange." Eighteen songs alternate between being creepy, funny, and gross. Three songs in the compilation can easily be used as movement songs. The first song "My Body Lies over the Ocean" is sung to "My Bonnie Lies over the Ocean." Jim Gill has a version of the traditional song on his CD *Jim Gill Sings Do Re Mi on His Toe Leg Knee* (Jim Gill Music, 1999). He instructs children to lift their arms up when they hear a word that begins with the letter B and then put them down the next time they hear the letter B. Throughout the song, children lift their arms up and down every time they hear the B sound. This same game can be applied to the monster version. Instead of having children raise their arms, try having them stand up or sit down every time they hear a word that starts with B. Children love this activity, especially when you start it slow, build to a medium speed, and finish fast. The second song, "If You're Scary and You Know It, Clap Your Paws," is a monster version of "If You're Happy and You Know It." You can extend the song by asking children to come up with several new verses. Possible verses are "If you're scary and you know it, stomp around," and "If you're scary and you know it, growl real loud." The third song, "Slither & Slink," is a good-bye song sung by creepy creatures to the tune of "Skinnamarink." Have children act out the song by adding movements to some of the words that are repeated. For example, when children hear the word *scare*, they can make a monster face. When they hear the word *stink*, they can hold their nose and wave their hand in front of their face.

Snoring Beauty, by Bruce Hale and illustrated by Howard Fine (Harcourt, 2007). In an offbeat, humorous version of *Sleeping Beauty*, King Gluteus and Queen Esophagus have a beautiful baby named Princess Drachmina Lofresca Malvolio Margarine. At her christening, the queen and king forget to invite Beebo the fairy, and as a result she curses the princess to die by a pie wagon. Another fairy, Tintinnitus, mishears the curse and says the princess will be turned into a sleeping dragon that can be revived only by a quince. When the princess turns sixteen, the curse is carried out, and the princess becomes a dragon who snores mightily in her sleep. How will a quince save the princess? This story is full of humor, wordplay, and unique vocabulary that children will enjoy. To make this story interactive, print out a sign with the word *snore*. As you read the story, hold up the sign to cue participants so they can snore with gusto like the princess dragon.

There Was an Old Monster! by Rebecca Emberley, Adrian Emberley, and Ed Emberley (Orchard Books, 2009). Based on the song "There Was an Old Lady Who Swallowed a Fly," this book shares the story of a monster that swallows a tick, ants, a lizard, and more. Adrian Emberley performs the song on Scholastic's website (www .scholastic.com/oldmonster). Her groovy adaption is fun to share with a group.

The 13 Nights of Halloween, by Guy Vasilovich (HarperCollins Children's Books, 2011). Start the countdown to Halloween with a song based on the tune "The Twelve Days of Christmas." A mummy gives a young girl gifts like a snake and "corpses caroling."

Twelve Haunted Rooms of Halloween, illustrated by Macky Pamintuan (Sterling Children's Books, 2011). Here's another twist on the "Twelve Days of Christmas." A young bear enters a haunted house and witnesses spiders, monsters, werewolves, jack-o'-lanterns and more. After reading the story, children can look through the book and search for 375 creatures.

What's in the Witch's Kitchen? **by Nick Sharratt (Candlewick Press, 2011).**
Find out what witches keep in their kitchen by lifting the flap on each two-page spread. Will it be something normal or something nasty?

BONUS TRACKS

"How to Move a Monster," from the recording *What a Ride!* by Eric Herman and the Invisible Band (Butter-Dog Records, 2009).
What do you do when a monster parks himself on top of your school? What will scare a monster away?

"Maybe the Monster," from the recording *Meltdown!* by Justin Roberts (Justin Roberts, 2006).
Justin Roberts sings about a monster underneath the bed. Could it be that the monster isn't as scary as people think?

"Monster in My Closet," from the recording *Radio Wayne*, by Wayne Brady (Walt Disney Records, 2011).
The monster in this closet isn't scary. This monster has a band and plays music all night long.

"Pumpkin," from the recording *Ladybug Music: Blue Collection*, by Ladybug Music (Ladybug Music, 2011).
Make different faces based on the emotions mentioned throughout the song.

"Purple People Eater," from the recording *Ranky Tanky*, by Rani Arbo and Daisy Mayhem (Mayhem Music, 2010).
Have you ever seen a purple people eater? If not, listen to the song to find out all about the creature.

NOTE

1. Kristyn Crow, *Bedtime at the Swamp,* n.p. HarperCollins, 2008. Used by permission of HarperCollins Publishers.

CHAPTER 12
ONCE UPON
A TIME

nce upon a time in a library far away, children listened to mixed-up fairy tales and silly nursery rhymes. To introduce this theme, ask children to name their favorite fairy tale, fairy-tale character, and villain. You could also list mixed-up fairy tales and nursery rhymes to see if children can figure out the correct name. For example:

Goldilocks and the Three Hares
Hey Diddle Doddle
Hickory Tickory Tock
Little Blue Riding Hood
Rapunzel and the Seven Dwarfs
The Three Teeny Pigs
The Tortoise and the Bear

The musical instrument for this theme is rhythm sticks. If you have access to rhythm sticks, there are several parts during the program when children can tap rhythms with them. If you don't have rhythm sticks, unsharpened pencils work, too.

PROGRAM PLAYLIST
- ▶ Opening Song: "Rum Sum Sum," from the recording *Buzz Buzz*, by Laurie Berkner
- ▶ Book: *Mind Your Manners, B. B. Wolf*, by Judy Sierra and illustrated by J. Otto Seibold

- ▶ Song: "The Billy Goats Gruff," from the recording *Imagination Generation*, by David Kisor
- ▶ Book: *Goldie and the Three Hares*, by Margie Palatini and illustrated by Jack E. Davis
- ▶ Song: "Fast and Slow," from the recording *Rocketship Run*, by the Laurie Berkner Band
- ▶ Book: *Hip & Hop, Don't Stop!*, by Jef Czekaj
- ▶ Song: "Throw It Out the Window," from the recording *Let's Go! Travel, Camp and Car Songs*, by Susie Tallman and Friends
- ▶ Book: *Dragon Pizzeria*, by Mary Morgan
- ▶ Activity: Fairy-Tale/Nursery-Rhyme Window
- ▶ Musical Instrument: Rhythm sticks

Opening Song

"Rum Sum Sum," from the recording *Buzz Buzz*, by Laurie Berkner (Two Tomatoes Records, 1998).

Follow Berkner's instructions for the actions that go along with the song or create your own. After playing the recording, turn it off and sing the song a second and third time going faster and faster, encouraging the group to join in and sing and perform the actions as quickly as possible. If you have rhythm sticks, children can do movements with the sticks instead of the hand motions. You can match certain words with particular actions, like tapping sticks together, tapping sticks on the ground, and making little circles in the air with the sticks.

Book

Mind Your Manners, B. B. Wolf, by Judy Sierra and illustrated by J. Otto Seibold (Alfred A. Knopf, 2007).

Miss Wonderly invites B. B. Wolf (a.k.a. Big Bad Wolf) to a very special event, the Annual Storybook Tea. B. B. Wolf's friends inform him that if he goes, he will have to be on his best behavior. To help him remember his manners, B. B. Wolf creates a song. Can he make it through the whole Storybook Tea without forgetting his manners? This book is great for a couple of reasons. First, the illustrations have a variety of fairy-tale references in them. For example, when B. B. Wolf checks his mailbox, he has several bills, including one for $3,900 to the House That Jack Built/Rebuilt for damage done to the two little pigs' homes. Second, during the part in the story when everyone is at the Storybook Tea, children can look at the illustrations and guess who all the participants are. Some, like Little Red Riding Hood and Humpty Dumpty, are from fairy tales and nursery rhymes, but others, like the Little Engine That Could and Elmer, are from famous picture books. It's fun to see if they can name all of them. Third, there's a part in the book when B. B. Wolf lets out a massive burp. That always gets a good laugh from the crowd. Finally, the story has a song. It's catchy, and you can sing it to a tune like the "Alphabet Song."

Song

"The Billy Goats Gruff," from the recording *Imagination Generation*, by David Kisor (Growing Sound, 2010).
Three billy goats, small, middle, and big, want to cross the bridge, but a troll has other plans. Kisor helps listeners act out the song. When the goats walk across the bridge, have children tap their rhythm sticks together to make the hoof sounds.

Book

***Goldie and the Three Hares*, by Margie Palatini and illustrated by Jack E. Davis (Katherine Tegen Books, 2011).**
Mama, Papa, and Baby Hare are settled in for a calm night when they hear a horrendous noise. When they look to see what happened, they notice Goldilocks. She fell down the stairs and injured her foot running from the bears. She has to stay with the hares. Goldilocks is an exacting, persnickety guest who needs just the right chair, pillow, and blanket. Can the Hares create a plan to persuade Goldie that it is time to go home?

Song

"Fast and Slow," from the recording *Rocketship Run*, by the Laurie Berkner Band (Two Tomatoes Records, 2008), or *The Best of the Laurie Berkner Band*, by the Laurie Berkner Band (Two Tomatoes Records, 2010).
Use this song to introduce the story about a tortoise and a hare. A rabbit wants to go fast, fast, fast. A turtle tells the rabbit that when you are fast,

you can overlook important things. After listening to this song, ask children what things the rabbit might miss if all he does is run fast.

Book

Hip & Hop, Don't Stop! by Jef Czekaj (Disney Hyperion Books, 2010).
In Slowjamz Swamp, Hip is a turtle who raps so slowly that his friends fall asleep. In Breakbeat Meadow, Hop is a bunny who raps so fast her friends can't understand what she's saying. One day they meet each other and become friends. They discover that they face the same challenge—others don't like their raps. Can Hip and Hop learn from each other? This is a new twist on the tortoise and hare story.

Song

"Throw It Out the Window," from the recording *Let's Go! Travel, Camp and Car Songs*, by Susie Tallman and Friends (Rock Me Baby Records, 2007).
This traditional song has a series of nursery rhymes in it. It's a silly nonsense song that is sometimes used at camp. Maria Muldaur has another version of the song, "Threw It out the Window," on her recording *Maria Muldaur's Barnyard Dance: Jug Band Music for Kids* (Music for Little People, 2010). You can extend the song by creating new verses with other nursery rhymes and fairy tales.

Book

Dragon Pizzeria, by Mary Morgan (Alfred A. Knopf, 2008).
Two dragons own Dragon Pizzeria. BeBop bakes the specialized concoctions, and Spike delivers them with speed to their neighbors in Fairy Tale Land. As BeBop cooks a giant pizza for Beanstalk Castle or three porridge pizzas for a bear family, he sings zippy rhymes. Each time a fairy-tale character places an order for a pizza, children can guess who it is and in which fairy tale the character stars.

Activity: Fairy-Tale/Nursery-Rhyme Window

Supplies:
▶ Construction paper
▶ White copy paper cut to represent a window

▶ Glue
▶ Crayons and markers

Directions:
Glue a piece of white paper onto construction paper so the construction paper makes a window frame. Talk to children about the song "Throw It Out the Window," and encourage them to draw a picture based on a fairy tale or nursery rhyme that was featured in the program or their own unique version of one. Play the song as they work on their art.

Musical Instrument
Rhythm Sticks

Supplies: rhythm sticks, pencils, or craft sticks
Directions:
▶ Demonstrate a short rhythm with the sticks, and have children mirror you.
▶ As the children become comfortable with simple rhythm patterns, extend the pattern so that it is a little bit longer.
▶ Work with the audience to develop a rhythm pattern for "Throw It Out the Window" or "Rum Sum Sum." Once the children have learned the pattern, turn on the music and have them play along.

BONUS BOOKS

The Cheese, by Margie Palatini and illustrated by Steve Johnson and Lou Fancher (Katherine Tegen Books, 2007).
We all know the song "The Farmer in the Dell" and the line "the cheese stands alone." When Rat sees a nice yellow chunk of cheese down in the meadow, he challenges the basis of the song. Why should the cheese be alone when he can keep it company and maybe sneak a nibble or two?

Hey Diddle Diddle, by Eve Bunting and illustrated by Mary Ann Fraser (Boyds Mills Press, 2011).
In this adapted nursery rhyme, it's not just the cat playing a musical instrument. The seal has a saxophone, the horse has a guitar, and the camel has a trumpet. Each animal plays a different instrument, and they are

all warming up for a concert. Although there are a variety of animals and instruments featured, there's still plenty of opportunity for children to come up with their own rhymes about unique animals and instruments.

The Library Gingerbread Man, by Dotti Enderle and illustrated by Colleen M. Madden (Upstart Books, 2010).

Use this book to introduce the Dewey decimal system. Who lives at 398.2? Gingerbread Man does, until he decides to leave home. He runs through the shelves passing different characters like the thesaurus (423.1) and a giraffe (599.638). He runs all the way to the biographies and finds himself stuck at the end of the shelves with an arctic fox (998), encouraging him to jump on his back. Will the fox eat Gingerbread Man, or will he be saved? And by whom?

The Little Red Pen, by Janet Stevens and Susan Stevens Crummel and illustrated by Janet Stevens (Harcourt Children's Books, 2011).

Loosely based on "The Little Red Hen," Little Red Pen has a stack of schoolwork to grade and needs help from stapler, highlighter, scissors, pencil, eraser, and pushpin (otherwise known as *chincheta*). All of Little Red Pen's friends hide from her, though, and she is left to do everything by herself, an impossible task. When she accidentally falls into the trash, her friends realize the importance of working together. The office products have their own personalities and are very funny. This would be a comical read-aloud for a school visit.

Marsupial Sue Presents "The Runaway Pancake," by John Lithgow and illustrated by Jack E. Davis (Simon & Schuster Books for Young Readers, 2005).

Marsupial Sue presents the play *The Runaway Pancake*. Auntie May cooks a pancake in her stove but is surprised to hear a voice from inside the oven. When she opens the door, a pancake escapes, singing a taunting song. As the pancake runs by a dog, a cow, and others, it sings the same song. John Lithgow retells the story on the accompanying CD. The song he sings for the runaway pancake is infectious and repetitive enough that children will want to join in and sing it.

The Pied Piper's Magic, by Steven Kellogg (Dial Books for Young Readers, 2009).

Not your traditional Pied Piper tale, an elf named Peterkin is given a magic pipe by a sad witch named Elbavol. The pipe makes music that sounds like letters. If Peterkin plays a song that spells out a word, the object that the word represents appears. He takes his newfound magic to a nearby village. The village, overrun by rats, has children but no parents because the grand duke is forcing the adults to work day and night. The grand duke has a reward for whoever can make the rats disappear, and Peterkin has an idea of how he can use his magic pipe to do that and to change the grand duke's hard heart.

Rapunzel and the Seven Dwarfs, by Willy Claflin and illustrated by James Stimson (August House, 2011).

Willy Claflin has a series of Maynard Moose tales with special moose language. This story is a combination of Rapunzel and Snow White and the Seven Dwarfs, retold with Maynard Moose's humor and unique word adaptations. A prince tries to help Punzel, but she mishears his instructions, and comical interactions ensue. Then eight or nine dwarfs join the story. Included is a CD with Claflin's version of the tale.

The Really Groovy Story of the Tortoise and the Hare, by Kristyn Crow and illustrated by Christina Forshay (Albert Whitman & Company, 2011).

Hare lives in the city. He's always on the run. Tortoise lives in the country and likes to relax with a book or float in the pool. When they see each other at the fair, Tortoise challenges Hare to a race. Hare knows he is going to win and accepts the challenge. During the race, Hare has a commanding lead so he decides to eat a snack, to play basketball, and to jam with his guitar. Hare wastes so much time that tortoise ends up ahead of him, and the winner of the race is no longer a sure thing.

Tell the Truth, B. B. Wolf, by Judy Sierra and illustrated by J. Otto Seibold (Alfred A. Knopf, 2010).

Miss Wonderly is at it again and invites B. B. Wolf to the library to tell the story of the three little pigs. B. B. Wolf spins the story trying to hide his villainous role, but the listeners implore B. B. Wolfe to be truthful. Just like in the first book, *Mind Your Manners, B. B. Wolf*, there are several songs that can be sung to a tune like "Mary Had a Little Lamb."

There Was an Odd Princess Who Swallowed a Pea, by Jennifer Ward and illustrated by Lee Calderon (Marshall Cavendish Children, 2011).

An odd princess swallows things like a pea, a wand, a glass slipper, and a rose in this fairy-tale adaptation of "There Was an Old Lady Who Swallowed a Fly."

BONUS TRACKS

"Hickory Dickory Dock," from the recording *Ladybug Music: Pink Collection*, by Ladybug Music (Ladybug Music, 2011).

Listen to a groovy interpretation of the nursery rhyme "Hickory Dickory Dock." The song also has a good drumbeat. You could use drums or rhythm sticks with the song to keep the beat.

"The Little Red Hen," from the recording *Fun and Games*, by Greg and Steve (Greg and Steve Productions, 2002).

Children can join in the chorus of the familiar story about a little hen who asks her barnyard friends for help planting, harvesting, and then making bread out of wheat.

"Lots of Little Pigs," from the recording *Buzz Buzz*, by Laurie Berkner (Two Tomatoes Records, 1998).

Berkner turns the story of the Three Little Pigs into a song. Pigs build a straw home, a stick home, and a brick home. When the wolves smell pigs, they visit each home in turn, trying to destroy them.

"Muffin Man," from the recording *Rock All Day Rock All Night*, by the Nields (Mercy House Productions, 2008).

The Nields adapt the nursery rhyme "Muffin Man" to include a variety of new verses involving different characters and breakfast foods. Children can join in and create their own verses, maybe the banana baby, the cereal cat, or the doughnut dog.

"There's a Cobbler," from the recording *Ladybug Music: Green Collection*, by Ladybug Music (Ladybug Music, 2011).

A cobbler fixes shoes of all sizes and for all types of feet: big, little, and even stinky.

"This Little Piggy," from the recording *Everyone Loves to Dance!* by Aaron Nigel Smith (Music for Little People, 2010).

Listen to this version of "This Little Piggy" with a new twist to the traditional lyrics.

"The Three Piggy Opera," from the recording *Singing All the Way Home*, by Liz Buchanan (Liz Buchanan, 2010).

Buchanan retells the Three Little Pigs' story. Special music plays whenever the Big Bad Wolf comes into the story.

CHAPTER 13
EARTH CELEBRATION

elebrate the earth with songs and stories about enjoying nature, planting gardens and trees, recycling and repurposing objects, and understanding that everyone can do something to help the earth.

Many musical instruments are made from natural items like wood, bamboo, gourds, and seeds. If you have musical instruments that are made from natural elements, bring them in and let children explore them. Ask them what materials they think the instrument is made of. For example, a wooden shaker is made of wood and dried beans.

During this program you can talk to children about reusing and repurposing items to make musical instruments. Hold up a plastic bottle and ask children what they think the plastic bottle can be transformed into. The final activity of the program gives children the chance to create and use a musical instrument made from a water bottle.

PROGRAM PLAYLIST

▶ Opening Song: "Sunny Day," from the recording *Sunny Day*, by Elizabeth Mitchell
▶ Book: *Whole World*, sung by Fred Penner and illustrated by Christopher Corr
▶ Song: "Roots & Shoots Everywhere," from the recording *Songs of Our World*, by Raffi
▶ Book: *Water, Weed, and Wait*, by Edith Hope Fine and Angela Demos Halpin and illustrated by Colleen Madden
▶ Song: "Earth Worm Disco," from the recording *Earth Worm Disco*, by Shira Kline

- ▶ Book: *Compost Stew: An A to Z Recipe for the Earth*, by Mary McKenna Siddals and illustrated by Ashley Wolff
- ▶ Song: "Under the Spreading Chestnut Tree," from *Three-Minute Tales: Stories from Around the World to Tell or Read When Time Is Short*, by Margaret Read MacDonald
- ▶ Book: *Stuff! Reduce, Reuse, Recycle*, by Steven Kroll and illustrated by Steve Cox
- ▶ Song: "Reduce Reuse Recycle & Rock!" from the recording Earth Worm Disco, by Shira Kline
- ▶ Activity: Earth Bingo
- ▶ Musical Instrument: Water-bottle maraca

Opening Song

"Sunny Day," from the recording *Sunny Day*, by Elizabeth Mitchell (Smithsonian Folkways Recordings, 2010).
This six-line song is repeated three times, the third time as a call-and-response. It touches on the growth cycle of a flower and the beauty of the sun. Use the song to introduce the theme and talk about celebrating the beauty of the earth.

Book

***Whole World*, sung by Fred Penner and illustrated by Christopher Corr (Barefoot Books, 2007).**
The accompanying CD has two versions of the song, one with lyrics and one without. The book has repetition, making the song easier to learn. Also, you can create actions for each of the verses, such as imitating fish by putting hands together and weaving them through the air, or forming trees by putting arms together and fanning fingers out. The author includes fun facts in the back about the earth, animals, and why it is so important for us to take care of our natural environment. Finally, you can extend the story by encouraging children to come up with their own verses.

Song

"Roots & Shoots Everywhere," from the recording *Songs of Our World*, by Raffi (Troubadour Music, 2008).

Before playing the song, ask children what roots and shoots are. Teach them to point to the ground when they hear the word *roots* and then to the sky when they hear *shoots*.

Book

Water, Weed, and Wait, by Edith Hope Fine and Angela Demos Halpin and illustrated by Colleen Madden (Tricycle Press, 2010).

Miss Marigold helps the students at Pepper Lane Elementary create their own school garden. The school's neighbor Mr. Barkley, otherwise known as Mr. Barks-a-Lot, is grumpy at first about the noise the children make as they prepare the school yard for the garden, but over time he, too, joins in the fun. The brightly colored illustrations vibrate with energy and will draw children into the joys of gardening. Transition to the next song by talking about the vegetables that the students plant in their garden and the things plants need to grow (soil, rain, and worms).

Song

"Earth Worm Disco," from the recording *Earth Worm Disco*, by Shira Kline (ShirLaLa, 2008).

Use this entertaining disco song to celebrate all the good things that worms provide the earth. Children will have the opportunity to pretend that they are a worm and dance.

Book

Compost Stew: An A to Z Recipe for the Earth, by Mary McKenna Siddals and illustrated by Ashley Wolff (Tricycle Press, 2010).

Introduce children to the idea of composting with a rhyming alphabet story. The author's note provides a brief explanation of composting, and the author uses the alphabet to describe all of the objects that can go into compost stew. The lovely collage illustrations have details children can explore.

Song

"Under the Spreading Chestnut Tree," from *Three-Minute Tales: Stories from Around the World to Tell or Read When Time Is Short,* **by Margaret Read MacDonald (August House Publishers, 2004).**

This action song can also be chanted. It is quick and fun, and each word has an action associated with it. Sing the song once with all the words and actions. Then repeat it several times, each time leaving another word blank and just doing the action. By the end, you will do the whole chant in silence with only the motions.

Book

Stuff! Reduce, Reuse, Recycle, **by Steven Kroll and illustrated by Steve Cox (Marshall Cavendish Children, 2009).**

Pinch's house overflows with piles and piles of stuff. One day his neighbors decide to have a garage sale to raise money to purchase a tree. They encourage Pinch to donate some of his things, but he doesn't want to let go of anything. After he sees his friends selling some of their items, he decides to bring out a few things. When he sells his stuff to other people, he notices that they love and appreciate his items more than he ever did. Use the story to talk about recycling and to brainstorm ways that children can recycle not just plastic and paper but also toys, books, and things they don't use but might be enjoyed by others in their neighborhood or school.

Song

"Reduce Reuse Recycle & Rock!" from the recording *Earth Worm Disco,* **by Shira Kline (ShirLaLa, 2008).**

Encourage children to join in singing the chorus. Later, while children are working on their instruments, play the remix version of "Reduce Reuse Recycle and Rock," by the Electric Junkyard Gamelan.

Activity
Earth Bingo

Directions: DLTK (www.dltk-cards.com/bingo) has a version of Earth Day Bingo. You can choose to have the bingo squares filled in with words and/or pictures. If you want to create your own bingo sheets, look for bingo generators online.

Give each child a bingo card. Call out different words, or if you are using pictures, describe them. If children have the word or the picture on their bingo card, they should mark it with something like pennies, pebbles, or beads. Once a child has marked a set number of squares in a row, he or she should yell, "Bingo!"

Musical Instrument
Water-Bottle Maraca

Supplies:
▶ Empty water bottles: 1 for each child
▶ Tape
▶ Dried beans, buttons, pennies, or other small items
▶ Craft sticks, straws, or pencils

Directions:
▶ Let children add different small items like beads, buttons, or beans to their water bottle so they can hear what sounds the items make.
▶ Attach the lid, and tape around the lid so that it is secure.
▶ Encourage children to experiment by tapping the bottle with a pencil or running a craft stick up and down the ridges of the bottle. What different sounds can they make with their instrument?

BONUS BOOKS

Gabby & Grandma Go Green, by Monica Wellington (Dutton Children's Books, 2011).
Gabby and Grandma have many different ways to be green. They start off by making their own cloth bags and use those bags to recycle plastic bottles. Then they visit the farmer's market to buy local food, and Gabby finishes the day with plans to make more bags with the leftover cloth. The author includes directions for sewing a cloth bag at the end of the book.

Joseph Had a Little Overcoat, by Simms Taback (Weston Woods, 2001).
Joseph leaves nothing to waste in this traditional tale. He wears his overcoat until it is "old and worn" and then transforms it into a jacket. From the jacket it becomes a vest, then a scarf, then a necktie, then a handker-

chief, and finally a button. The Weston Woods version comes with a CD that includes the song "I Had a Little Overcoat."

Nibbles: A Green Tale, by Charlotte Middleton (Marshall Cavendish Children, 2010).

Nibbles is a guinea pig that *loves* dandelion leaves. Unfortunately, too many animals eat them. Pretty soon all of the dandelions are gone, all except for one by Nibbles's window. Nibbles really, really wants to eat it, but he realizes he must find a way to turn that one dandelion into many. He visits the library to research dandelions and formulates a plan to save them from extinction.

Surf War! by Margaret Read MacDonald and illustrated by Geraldo Valério (August House Littlefolk, 2009).

What happens when Whale demands that Sandpiper stay out of the ocean because, of course, the ocean is only for whales? What happens when Sandpiper declares that there are more sandpipers than whales and the ocean belongs to them, too? A surf war erupts, with each animal calling in reinforcements to prove its point. Before you know it, the sea is full of whales, and the beach is teeming with birds. Whale gets so angry he tells the other whales to eat up the land. The sandpiper responds by encouraging the birds to drink up the sea, leaving fish and crabs and starfish exposed to the sun. Finally, Sandpiper and Whale realize the destruction they are causing. In this folktale from the Marshall Islands, we are reminded that our actions have repercussions on the environment and that everything is interconnected.

Tweedle Dee Dee, by Charlotte Voake (Candlewick Press, 2008).

Based on the traditional folk song "The Green Leaves Grew All Around," a boy and girl discover a tree, and in that tree is a very special surprise. The endpapers contain the musical score.

Wendel's Workshop, by Chris Riddell (Katherine Tegen Books, 2010).

Wendel enjoys inventing contraptions. Sometimes they work and sometimes they don't. When an invention doesn't work, he throws it out on the trash heap. One day he decides to invent a robot to clean his house. The first robot, Clunk, doesn't work according to plan, so Wendel throws it out. The second robot, Wendelbot, works so well that the robot throws out anything that prevents the house from being tidy, including Wendel. With the help of Clunk, Wendel realizes that he can reuse all of the junk on the trash heap and create an army to defeat Wendelbot.

BONUS TRACKS

"Do You Hear the Birds Singing?" from the recording *Mind of My Own*, by Frances England (Frances England, 2010).

This song encourages taking time to hear and feel and experience nature around you.

"Future Man, Future Lady," from the recording *Family Time*, by Ziggy Marley with Laurie Berkner (Tuff Gong Worldwide, 2009).

The song reminds children that they have the future of the planet in their hands.

"Good Garbage," from the recording *This Pretty Planet*, by Tom Chapin (Sony Music Entertainment, 2000).

Listen and find out what *biodegradable* means and why some items make good garbage and some items make bad garbage. The whole CD focuses on environmental issues and is nice to use as background music before and after the program.

"The Great Outdoors," from the recording *All Around Ralph's World*, by Ralph Covert (Bar/None Records, 2010).

This song encourages children to explore the great outdoors.

"The Green Grass Grows All Around," from the recording *Ranky Tanky*, by Rani Arbo and Daisy Mayhem (Mayhem Music, 2010).

This peppy, cumulative folk song starts with a hole, then dirt, then roots, then a tree, and so on. Another version of the song, "Green Grass Grew All Around," can be found on *Stories & Songs for Little Children*, by Pete Seeger (High Windy Audio, 1995).

"Humungous Tree," from the recording *Snacktime!* by Barenaked Ladies (Desperation Records, 2008).

Barenaked Ladies sings a song about the importance of trees.

"Plant a Garden," from the recording *Play!* by Milkshake (Milkshake Music, 2006).

A little girl and her friends transform a barren lot into a lovely garden.

"Reduce, Reuse, Recycle," from the recording *Going Green! with Dr. Jean*, by Dr. Jean Feldman and Dr. Holly Karapetkova (Progressive Music, 2009).

Dr. Jean uses music to help students learn different concepts like what the words *reduce, reuse,* and *recycle* mean. Other songs on the CD deal with subjects like endangered animals, Earth Day, picking up litter, and turning off electronics. Free activities and printable lyrics for her CD can be found on her website (http://drjean.org/html/lyrics/lyricsGoingGreen.pdf).

"What a Wonderful World," featuring Erin Dangar, from the recording *Grandkid Rock*, by Daddy a Go Go (Boyd's Tone Records, 2011).
Written by George David Weiss and Bob Thiele and performed most notably by Louis Armstrong, Daddy a Go Go's rock version of "What a Wonderful World" is another great song to use to end the program. If you are looking for the Louis Armstrong version, it can be found on the recording *Jazz for Kids: Sing, Clap, Wiggle and Shake* (Verve Music Group, 2004).

CHAPTER 14
GAME TIME

t's the beauty of everyone singing "The Star-Spangled Banner," the excitement of belting out "Take Me Out to the Ball Game" during the seventh-inning stretch, and the thrill of the fight song played when the game is tied with thirty seconds left. Both music and sports pull on our emotions and passions. Celebrate game time with books, rhymes, and songs based on several different sports, or pull out material to focus on one particular sport like baseball or soccer. As an introduction to the program, ask children what their favorite sport and sports team is. Bring in sporting equipment and see if they can guess which sport each item represents.

PROGRAM PLAYLIST

▶ Opening Song: "The Irrational Anthem," from the recording *Jim Gill's Irrational Anthem and More Salutes to Nonsense*, by Jim Gill

▶ Book: *Going, Going, Gone! and Other Silly Dilly Sports Songs*, by Alan Katz and illustrated by David Catrow

▶ Book: *Dino-Basketball*, by Lisa Wheeler and illustrated by Barry Gott

▶ Book: *Take Me Out to the Ball Game*, by Jack Norworth and illustrated by Amiko Hirao

▶ Song: "Baseball Time"

▶ Book: *Sergio Saves the Game!* by Edel Rodriguez

▶ Song: "Sports Song"

▶ Song: "Sports Dance," from the recording *On the Move*, by Greg and Steve

▶ Activity: "Pass the Ball," from *Wee Sing Games, Games, Games*, by Pamela Conn Beall and Susan Hagen Nipp and illustrated by Nancy Spence Klein
▶ Musical Instrument: Paper-plate cymbals

Opening Song

"The Irrational Anthem," from the recording *Jim Gill's Irrational Anthem and More Salutes to Nonsense*, by Jim Gill (Jim Gill Music, 2001).
Warm up the audience with an action song that will keep everyone loose and limber. Children start with one motion and during each succeeding verse add another movement until the end, when they are doing six actions at the same time.

Book

Going, Going, Gone! and Other Silly Dilly Sports Songs, by Alan Katz and illustrated by David Catrow (Margaret K. McElderry Books, 2009).
Fourteen funny sports songs like "Ode to Umps and Refs" and "On Top of the Bleachers" are sung to traditional tunes like "Home on the Range" and "On Top of Old Smokey." Pick your favorite song to introduce the book, or try the basketball tune "We're Choosing up Sides," sung to "The Wheels on the Bus." This tune brings to life the nervous feeling a child experiences when waiting to be chosen for a team.

Book

Dino-Basketball, by Lisa Wheeler and illustrated by Barry Gott (Carolrhoda Books, 2011).
It's the herbivorous Grass Clippers versus the carnivorous Meat team. This rollicking, rhyming basketball story follows the thrills of a March Madness basketball game. Who will win? Other books in the series include *Dino-Hockey* (Carolrhoda Books, 2007), *Dino-Soccer* (Carolrhoda Books, 2009), and *Dino-Baseball* (Carolrhoda Books, 2010).

Book

Take Me Out to the Ball Game, **by Jack Norworth and illustrated by Amiko Hirao (Imagine, 2011).**

It's the seventh-inning stretch. Have everyone stand up, do arm stretches, touch their toes, turn around, and join in singing "Take Me Out to the Ball Game." Carly Simon performs the song on the accompanying CD. The large action illustrations capture the excitement of a baseball game.

Song

"Baseball Time"

Sung to the tune "The More We Get Together":

The more we throw the baseball, the baseball, the baseball
Action: Pretend to wind up and throw the baseball
The more we throw the baseball, the better we will be
If you throw and I catch
And I throw and you catch
The more we throw the baseball, the better we will be.

The more we swing the bat, the bat, the bat
Action: Get in a hitter's stance and swing an imaginary bat
The more we swing the bat, the better we will be
If you swing the bat and I hit the ball
And I swing the bat and you hit the ball
The more we swing the bat, the better we will be.

The more we run the bases, the bases, the bases
Action: Run in place
The more we run the bases, the better we will be.
If you run a base and I steal a base
And I run a base and you steal a base
The more we run the bases, the better we will be.

The more we cheer for the baseball team, the baseball team, the baseball team,
Action: Cup hands around mouth like yelling or clap hands
The more we cheer for the baseball team, the better they will be.
If you cheer real loud and I clap my hands

And I cheer real loud and you clap your hands
The more we cheer for the baseball team, the better they will be.

Book

Sergio Saves the Game! by Edel Rodriguez (Little, Brown and Company Books for Young Readers, 2009).

Penguin soccer star Sergio has all the moves and can score like a champion, but only when he's dreaming in his sleep. When he wakes up, he is a klutz and ends up scoring for the opposing team. His parents suggest that he switch to the goalie position. Sergio tries his best but has the same problems. His coach tells him to keep practicing and Sergio does. Will his practice pay off when Sergio's team plays for the championship against the Seagulls?

Song

"Sports Song"
Sung to the tune "Frère Jacques":

Hockey player, hockey player
Slap the puck, slap the puck
Squeeze it past the goalie, squeeze it past the goalie
Win the game, win the game.

Soccer player, soccer player
Head the ball, head the ball,
Pass it to your teammate, pass it to your teammate
Watch her score, watch her score.

Football player, football player
Throw the ball, throw the ball
Catch it midair, catch it midair
Run it in, run it in.

Team player, team player
Make new friends, make new friends
Practice everyday, practice everyday
And have some fun and have some fun.

Song

"Sports Dance," from the recording *On the Move*, by Greg and Steve (Young Heart Music, 2000).

Greg and Steve introduce a variety of sports dances (basketball, jump rope, football, hula hoop, baseball, and hopscotch) and encourage children to act out the moves.

Activity

"Pass the Ball," from *Wee Sing Games, Games, Games*, by Pamela Conn Beall and Susan Hagen Nipp and illustrated by Nancy Spence Klein (Price Stern Sloan, 2002).

Have children sit in a circle, and play the song on the CD that accompanies the book. Give children a ball, instructing them to pass it from one to another until they hear a musical cue that directs them to send the ball the other way. The changes in tempo and the frequency of cues make this activity more difficult than it originally seems. Children will laugh as they try to keep the directions straight and the ball from hitting the ground.

Musical Instrument
Paper-Plate Cymbals

Supplies: heavy-duty paper or plastic plates
Directions:

- ▶ Give each child 2 plates.
- ▶ Ask them to decorate the plates as desired.
- ▶ Have them tap the back side of the two plates together to make rhythmic sounds, like mascots make when they walk around with drums and lead chants at sporting events.
- ▶ Play a fight song from the local high school or college, and have children use the paper plates to keep the rhythm. If the school has a well-known chant, share that as well.

BONUS BOOKS

All Access, by Aimee Crawford (Time Books, 2010).

Ever wonder how the size of your hand compares to the size of Shaquille O'Neal's hand, or how they turn a hockey stadium into a basketball arena, or the meaning of the images on a hockey goalie's helmet? If so, this book is for you. Share some of these facts with children and then let them look through the book after the program. There's a little something for every sports fan.

Bats at the Ballgame, by Brian Lies (Houghton Mifflin Books for Children, 2010).

Finally, it's nighttime and the bats prepare for an evening of baseball. Children will love the detailed illustrations and wordplay. A concession worker sells "moth-dogs" and Cricket Jack. During the seventh-inning stretch, the bats sing their own special version of "Take Me Out to the Ball Game." The grounds crew stripes the field with powdered sugar, and they rake the mound with a fork. Besides all of the fun little details in the drawings, the story portrays a thrilling game, down to the last throw in the final inning.

Bat's Big Game, by Margaret Read MacDonald and illustrated by Eugenia Nobati (Albert Whitman and Company, 2008).

In this soccer game it's the Animals versus the Birds. When Bat comes to play, he decides to join the Animals because they look athletic. The Animals are unsure about Bat because he has wings, but Bat sweet talks them into letting him join their team. When the Animals start to lose, Bat figures he has joined the losing team and switches sides. The Birds aren't quite sure about Bat, but he sweet talks them into playing on their side. When both teams realize that Bat is going back and forth trying to play on the winning team, they tell him that he can't be on either of their teams. Bat learns the hard way that a good player perseveres through the difficult times, and a player who cares only about winning doesn't make a good teammate.

Gunner, Football Hero, by James E. Ransome (Holiday House, 2010).

Gunner doesn't look like your typical football player, but he has a great arm that lands him on the team as third-string quarterback. When Gunner gets a chance to play in a game, can he prove that he's a good football player?

If I Were a Jungle Animal, by Amanda Ellery and illustrated by Tom Ellery (Simon and Schuster Books for Young Readers, 2009).

This book is for all those children who daydream in the outfield. Morton is in the backfield during a baseball game, and he has a very hard time paying attention. His imagination runs wild as he envisions himself on an adventure in a jungle as a lion, monkey, zebra, and more. But will he wake up in time to get the ball?

Not All Princesses Dress in Pink, **by Jane Yolen and Heidi E. Y. Stemple and illustrated by Anne-Sophie Lanquetin (Simon & Schuster Books for Young Readers, 2010).**

Not your stereotypical princesses, these girls play baseball wearing the typical uniform, with an added accessory of a crown. Others play soccer or use power tools or ride bikes.

Soccer Hour, **by Carol Nevius and illustrated by Bill Thomson (Marshall Cavendish, 2011).**

This rhyming story features the hard work and fun of soccer practice. Large illustrations are perfect to share with a group. Other books in the series include *Baseball Hour* (Marshall Cavendish, 2008) and *Karate Hour* (Marshall Cavendish, 2004).

Splinters, **by Kevin Sylvester (Tundra Books, 2010).**

In a Cinderella adaptation, Cindy, nicknamed "Splinters," is a phenomenal hockey player, but her coach and her coach's daughters don't let her play. Since she sits on the bench so much, they've nicknamed her "Splinters." When there is an all-star hockey team tryout, Cindy wants the opportunity to skate in front of the head coach Charmaine Prince. She knows that her coach won't let her. That's when her fairy goaltender appears and helps her make the tryouts. Can Cindy make an impression on the coach?

BONUS TRACKS

"Baseball," from the recording *Play!* by Milkshake (Milkshake Music, 2007).
The Milkshake band sings about the joy of playing baseball.

"Baseball Dreams," from the recording *At the Bottom of the Sea,* by Ralph's World (Walt Disney Records, 2006).
Ralph Covert sings about his baseball dreams of being a Cubs player.

"The Sports Song," from the recording *Grandkid Rock,* by Daddy a Go Go (Boyd's Tone Records, 2011).
A child has fun playing on the baseball, football, and soccer fields.

CHAPTER 15
TASTY TUNES
AND TALES

egin by asking children to talk about their favorite food. Share some fun facts from books like *The Scoop on Ice Cream*, by Catherine Ipcizade (Capstone Press, 2012). Tell some jokes or riddles from books like *The Funny Food Joke Book*, by Sean Connolly and Kay Barnham (Windmill Books, 2012). Follow up with the program playlist that features songs and stories about soup, sweet potatoes, spaghetti, and sweets (as well as a few foods that don't start with *s*). There are enough resources in the bonus sections for additional programs on soup, snacks, or desserts.

PROGRAM PLAYLIST

▶ Opening Song: "Aiken Drum"
▶ Book: *Fandango Stew*, by David Davis and illustrated by Ben Galbraith
▶ Song: "Soup, Soup," from the recording *Banjo to Beatbox*, by Cathy and Marcy with Christylez Bacon
▶ Book: *The Gigantic Sweet Potato*, by Dianne de Las Casas and illustrated by Marita Gentry
▶ Song: "Bananas," from the recording *Jim Gill Presents Music Play for Folks of All Stripes*, by Jim Gill
▶ Book: *On Top of Spaghetti*, by Paul Brett Johnson with lyrics by Tom Glazer
▶ Song: "Fried Ham," from the book and CD *Lisa Loeb's Silly Sing-Along: The Disappointing Pancake and Other Zany Songs*, by Lisa Loeb and illustrated by Ryan O'Rourke

- ▶ Book: *Whopper Cake*, by Karma Wilson and illustrated by Will Hillenbrand
- ▶ Song: "The Cookie Jar Chant" and "The Cookie Jar Song," from the recording *Camp Lisa*, by Lisa Loeb
- ▶ Activity: "All around the Kitchen," from the recording *American Folk, Game & Activity Songs for Children*, by Pete Seeger
- ▶ Musical Instrument: Kitchen percussion

Opening Song

"Aiken Drum"

This song asks for participants to come up with food items that represent different clothing or body parts. Here are the basic lyrics:

First verse:
There was a man lived in the moon, in the moon, in the moon.
There was a man lived in the moon and his name was Aiken Drum.

Chorus:
And he played upon a ladle, a ladle, a ladle.
He played upon a ladle and his name was Aiken Drum.

Second verse:
And his hair was made of _____, of _____, of _____.
His hair was made of _____, and his name was Aiken Drum.

You can create as many verses as you want. Children are very inventive with this song. One group of mine decided that Aiken's mouth was made of a banana, his eyes of strawberries, and his belly button of sushi. You can draw Aiken as you go, too.

Book

Fandango Stew, by David Davis and illustrated by Ben Galbraith (Sterling, 2011).
Two cowboys, Luis and Slim, mosey into the town of Skinflint with nothing but a fandango bean, hungry stomachs, and a song. Townsfolk start off alternating between suspicion and skepticism of the visitors and want them out of town. Luis and Slim insist that they can create the best-tasting

stew with one fandango bean. With a little sweet talking they set about to prove themselves to the town. The story begins with Luis and Slim as the only two who sing a song about fandango stew. As each person adds a special ingredient, that person also joins in singing the song, so in the end the whole town is singing together. You can approach this song in one of two ways. You can have everyone sing the song each time at the same volume, or you can start by having the children sing the song quietly, almost a whisper, and then get a little bit louder each time until the end, when the whole town sings the song together.

Song

"Soup, Soup," from the recording *Banjo to Beatbox*, by Cathy and Marcy with Christylez Bacon (Community Music, 2009).
What's your favorite soup? This song lists the many varieties of soup. After each line there is an easy repetition that children can join in on. One of the performers plays the spoons, which makes this a good song to use if you are teaching children how to play the spoons.

Book

The Gigantic Sweet Potato, by Dianne de Las Casas and illustrated by Marita Gentry (Pelican, 2010).
In this version of the Russian folktale "The Giant Turnip," Ma Farmer loves to garden and eat the fresh produce she grows. When she longs for sweet potato pie, she determines to grow sweet potatoes. The problem occurs when it is time to collect the sweet potato to make her pie. No matter how much effort she exerts to pull it out of the ground, the sweet potato remains stuck. There's a little repeated phrase that each person and animal says when they join the line to help pull out the sweet potato. Try adding a tune to the chant, and teach it to children so that they can sing along. Included is a recipe for sweet potato pie and interesting facts about sweet potatoes and how to grow them.

Song

"Bananas," from the recording *Jim Gill Presents Music Play for Folks of All Stripes*, by Jim Gill (Jim Gill Music, 2011).
This is an energetic action song that ends with an opportunity for children to do a crazy dance.

Book

On Top of Spaghetti, by Paul Brett Johnson, with lyrics by Tom Glazer (Scholastic Press, 2006).

Oh, no! Yodeler's restaurant Yodeler Jones's Spaghetti Emporium and Musicale lost all of his business when the Fried Fritter Fricassee restaurant opened. Now he's focused on creating an unequaled meatball. The problem occurs when somebody sneezes and the meatball flies out of his restaurant. As he chases after it, he sings the familiar tune "On Top of Spaghetti." Join in the fun by singing the song and sneezing along with the story. Lyrics and music are included at the end of the book.

Song

"Fried Ham," from the book and CD *Lisa Loeb's Silly Sing-Along: The Disappointing Pancake and Other Zany Songs,* by Lisa Loeb and illustrated by Ryan O'Rourke (Sterling Children's Books, 2011).

Loeb has a variety of food-themed songs in this book and accompanying CD. "Fried Ham" is great because each time it is sung, it's performed in a different voice, like a cowboy voice and an opera voice. Another food song is "The Disappointing Pancake." In this song a rock-hard pancake is too tough to be a breakfast food, but he leaves home and finds ways to help people.

Book

Whopper Cake, by Karma Wilson and illustrated by Will Hillenbrand (Margaret K. McElderry Books, 2007).

For Grandma's birthday, Granddad has it in mind that a small chocolate cake won't do, so he supersizes the recipe. Instead of cups of sugar, he adds bags. Instead of a regular bowl, he utilizes a truck bed. There's nothing simple and ordinary about his cake. In the end, though, will Grandma like her whopper cake?

Song

"The Cookie Jar Chant" and "The Cookie Jar Song," from the recording *Camp Lisa,* by Lisa Loeb (Furious Rose Productions, 2008).

Loeb performs this traditional camp chant with a group of children. Have children join in and snap their fingers and clap their hands during the rhythmic chant. The performers ad-lib and name many types of cookies. Afterward, ask children if they can think of any cookies not mentioned in the song. Loeb follows the chant with a mellow musical version that explains who really stole the cookies.

Activity

"All Around the Kitchen," from the recording *American Folk, Game & Activity Songs for Children,* **by Pete Seeger (Smithsonian Folkways Recordings, 2000).**

Arrange the group in a circle and have them walk until they hear Seeger instruct them to stop and do an action. Then resume walking until they are instructed to stop again and do another action. Dan Zanes has a version of the game on his recording *Family Dance* (Festival Five Records, 2001). As children move in a circle, you can have them dance or walk any way that you want. You can have them follow the leader and do different hand motions or walk like an Egyptian or bunny hop.

Musical Instrument
Kitchen Percussion

Supplies:
- ▶ Kitchen objects like spoons, spatulas, pots, pans, sponges, cookie sheets, and anything else that will make an interesting sound

Directions:
- ▶ Introduce a variety of kitchen objects and experiment with the sounds that they make. For example, bring in some metal spoons and let children experiment with playing the spoons. Bring in pots and pans, pie plates, and spatulas to make drum sounds. Even clean scrubbers on a cookie sheet will make an interesting noise.
- ▶ Let children pick an object or two to experiment with.
- ▶ Have children play along to a song like "Coming Down with the Lemonade" from the recording *Ladybug Music: Purple Collection* (Ladybug Music, 2010). Another one for rhythm instruments is "Bowl of Cherries," by Rhythm Child, from the recording *Picnic Playground: Musical Treats from Around the World* (Putumayo World Music, 2009).

BONUS BOOKS

The Cazuela That the Farm Maiden Stirred, **by Samantha R. Vamos and illustrated by Rafael López (Charlesbridge, 2011).**

Created using the same cumulative structure as the traditional rhyme, "The House That Jack Built," this story is of a young woman who begins with a pot, or *cazuela*. Different farm animals add ingredients to the pot until the end result of rice pudding, *arroz con leche*, is achieved. Some of the nouns are mentioned in English once and then replaced with their Spanish counterpart. Because this is a cumulative story, many of the words are repeated several times, helping children learn new Spanish words and what they represent.

Cooking with Henry and Elliebelly, **by Carolyn Parkhurst and illustrated by Dan Yaccarino (Feiwel and Friends, 2010).**

Henry pretend plays that he is a chef on his own cooking show, along with his younger sister and cooking assistant Elliebelly. Elliebelly is two, though, and has specific ideas for what they should do during the show, ideas that don't match up with Henry's. The story is told in dialogue and has three distinct voices, Elliebelly, Henry, and their mother, who is in the other room and never pictured. Since Elliebelly is so young, she speaks in demonstrative short sentences or phrases and can't understand why Henry doesn't want to exchange his chef's hat for a pirate's hat or why she can't add pizza to the waffle batter. Henry tries to reason with Elliebelly but finds out that doesn't quite work with a toddler. Older siblings will relate to the dynamics between big brother and little sister.

The Donut Chef, **by Bob Staake (Golden Books, 2008).**

A doughnut chef opens a bakery that becomes instantly popular until competition moves in next door. The two chefs battle against each other, trying to fashion the most unique doughnuts. They are so focused on the competition that they lose sight of the doughnuts and their customers until one little girl asks for a type of doughnut that changes everything.

Easy as Pie, **by Cari Best and illustrated by Melissa Sweet (Farrar, Straus and Giroux, 2010).**

Do you like to watch cooking shows? Jacob does. He loves *Baking with Chef Monty* and knows all of Chef Monty's rules for pies. He decides to bake a pie even though his family wants to go out to eat. As he cooks, he runs through the rules. For example, he reminds himself of the importance of paying attention to the process of baking. No distractions! Jacob likes to sing while he bakes. At one point he performs his own version of "Pat-a-Cake." By the end of the story Chef Jacob has developed a few baking rules of his own. Ask children if they have baked anything with their family or friends. Follow up by asking them if they have any baking rules they follow.

The Gingerbread Man Loose in the School, by Laura Murray and illustrated by Mike Lowery (G. P. Putnam's Sons, 2011).

A classroom mixes and bakes a gingerbread man. When the students leave for recess, the lonely gingerbread man is determined to find them. He journeys throughout the school halls, visiting the gym teacher, the art instructor, and even the principal, all along the way singing a song about finding his friends.

The Haunted Hamburger and Other Ghostly Stories, by David LaRochelle and illustrated by Paul Meisel (Dutton Children's Books, 2011).

Included in the book are three scary (well, mostly funny) ghost stories. Share all three, or just read the "The Haunted Hamburger." Ghost Nell believes she is the best at anything and everything, so when a friend challenges her superiority and says that the Haunted Hamburger is better at things than she is, she sets out to prove her wrong. Find out what makes the hamburger so frightening.

How to Make a Cherry Pie and See the USA, by Marjorie Priceman (Alfred A. Knopf, 2008).

What if the cooking store is closed and you don't have the tools you need to make a cherry pie? What's left to do? Travel the United States and see where cotton is made for the pot holders and where clay is found for the mixing bowl. Crisscross the country learning interesting facts about the states and their natural resources.

If You Give a Dog a Donut, by Laura Numeroff and illustrated by Felicia Bond (Balzer + Bray, 2011).

Numeroff's "If You Give . . ." books are perfect for prop stories. They are sequence stories that refer to a variety of objects and actions. In this one, a dog eats a doughnut. The doughnut makes him thirsty. When he runs out of apple juice, he looks for more apples. Apples remind him of baseball. The story continues in this manner until it comes full circle. Gather small objects for your props. Discount stores and garage sales are great places to find props. A call out to coworkers can help. Put your props in a brown lunch bag or lunch box and pull them out as you share the story.

You can also give each child a prop and have the child bring the prop up when he or she hears it mentioned in the story. Two opportunities in the book allow participants to join in and do a special dance and talk like a pirate.

Oscar and the Very Hungry Dragon, by Ute Krause (North-South Books, 2010).

A starving dragon wants to eat a princess, but the town doesn't have a princess, so they give him Oscar. Oscar is a smart young boy, and he encourages the dragon to wait until he is nice and plump. The dragon agrees and brings him what he needs to cook delectable meals. The boy tempts the dragon with all manners of aromatic, eye-appealing tasty food, but dragons eat humans, not food made by humans. Will Oscar be able to outsmart the dragon? For a program about clever children who use their wits and food to outsmart witches, dragons, and ghosts, pair this book with *Hansel & Gretel*, by the Brothers Grimm, retold by Amy Ehrlich and illustrated by Susan Jeffers (Dutton Children's Books, 2011), and *Boy Dumplings*, by Ying Chang Compestine and illustrated by James Yamasaki (Holiday House, 2009).

The Princess of Borscht, by Leda Schubert and illustrated by Bonnie Christensen (Roaring Brook Press, 2011).

After Ruthie visits her grandma in the hospital, she comes up with a plan to make her grandma's favorite soup, borscht. The problem is she doesn't know her grandma's secret recipe. Ruthie's neighbors all have their own recipes and believe they cook the best borscht. With so many cooks in the kitchen, will Ruthie be able to make a soup that pleases her grandma?

The Real Story of Stone Soup, by Ying Chang Compestine and illustrated by Stéphane Jorisch (Dutton Children's Books, 2007).

In this Chinese folktale, a fisherman tells a story of creating soup by adding hot stones to water. He begins by talking about three young boys who he hired to help him fish. Although he considers them laid back and not so smart, as the story progresses, it becomes more and more evident that the fisherman isn't as clever as he thinks and that he likes to nap instead of work. The three boys take that knowledge and play a trick on the fisherman. So how is this soup made? Not in a pot and not with food given by neighbors. Share the book to talk with children about a new way of making stone soup.

The Runaway Wok, by Ying Chang Compestine and illustrated by Sebastià Serra (Dutton Children's Books, 2011).

A young boy named Ming purchases an old wok from the local market instead of bringing home food for his poor family. His parents are not impressed. The wok, though, is a magical wok that sings and travels. It rolls to the home of a selfish rich family. When Mrs. Li sees the wok, she decides it's perfect to house the food for her Chinese New Year dinner, so she has servants fill it up with rice and dumplings and noodles. Once the wok is full, it rolls back to Ming's home and surprises Ming's family. When the wok is empty, it rolls back to the rich family. Back and forth the magic wok goes, taking from the rich family and helping the poor. The wok sings two songs, one on his way to the rich man's family and one on his way to the poor man's home. Children can join in and chant the two-line songs.

A Soup Opera, **by Jim Gill and illustrated by David Moose (Jim Gill Books, 2009).**

A man has ordered onion soup, but he isn't able to eat it. He talks to the waiter, who brings the cook, who brings a police officer, and so on. All ask the gentleman what's wrong, and he replies in the same way that he isn't able to eat the soup. When the characters speak, they communicate in an expressive operatic voice. The book has an accompanying CD with tracks to be played while the story is dramatized. As the CD suggests, you can play one track and hear an orchestrated version of Gill and friends telling the story. Tracks 2–35 are accompaniment tracks with the operatic lines included. If you choose this option, you can read the majority of the story and lip-synch the operatic singing parts. Tracks 36–70 only have the musical accompaniment, so you can read the story and do the operatic lines. With a few props and a little practice, this story is fun for teens to share with a younger audience as a reader's theater.

BONUS TRACKS

"Apples and Bananas," from the recording *Ladybug Music: Green Collection*, by Ladybug Music (Ladybug Music, 2011).

Practice your vowel sounds while singing the song. Each verse features a different vowel, and all the vowels in the song are changed to that specific one. For example, one verse uses the long *a* and another verse only has the long *i* sound. This particular version of the song has a Caribbean feel to it. Keith Urban also has a version on *Country Goes Raffi* (Rounder, 2001).

***Buzz Buzz*, by Laurie Berkner (Two Tomatoes Records, 1998).**

This album has three songs that talk about food. "Ice Cream Cone" mentions some ice-cream flavors and the different ways to eat an ice-cream cone. "The Valley of Vegetables" is a song about vegetables and the noise you make when you eat them. What does it sound like when popcorn is calling you? Find out by listening to "Popcorn Calling Me."

"Eat Every Bean and Pea on Your Plate," from the recording *Grandkid Rock,* **by Daddy a Go Go (Boyd's Tone Records, 2011).**
Learn about the healthy foods that you should be eating (including beans and peas).

Giggling and Laughing: Silly Songs for Kids **(Music for Little People, 2010).**
The MFLP Players perform "A Peanut on the Railroad Track," a short song that describes what happens to a peanut when it rests on a railroad track. The Persuasions sing a soulful "On Top of Spaghetti," in which someone sneezes and a meatball rolls away and is lost.

Going on a Picnic, **by the Dreamtree Shakers (Dreamtree Shakers, 2011).**
There's nothing like "Ants on a Log" for a yummy snack. Or imagine a land of candy and sweets in the "Big Rock Candy Mountain."

"Peanut Butter & Jelly," from the recording *Fun and Games,* **by Greg and Steve (Greg & Steve Productions, 2002).**
How do you make peanut butter and jelly? Act out each step in making a favorite childhood staple.

"Pease Porridge Hot," from the recording *Ladybug Music: Yellow Collection,* **by Ladybug Music (Ladybug Music, 2010).**
Listen to a mariachi version of the traditional "Pease Porridge Hot" with a few Spanish words woven into the recording.

Picnic Playground: Musical Treats from Around the World **(Putumayo World Music, 2009).**
"Eat Like a Rainbow," by Jay Mankita from the United States, extols the virtues of eating foods that are the colors of the rainbow. "Ice Cream," by Asheba from Trinidad, describes different ways to eat ice cream and how ice cream makes people feel. "Beautiful Day," by Kheswa from South Africa, explains what makes the day beautiful, including the smells of food wafting through the air and the taste of papayas. "Bowl of Cherries," by Rhythm Child from the United States, sings about the joy of eating cherries. Pass out shakers or tambourines, and children can join in and keep the rhythm of the song. "Shoo Fly Pie," by Johnny Bregar from the United States, talks about the mysterious food shoofly pie and why it is so amazing. "Let's Bake Cookies," by Maggie G. from Canada, depicts the process of baking cookies. "Milch," by Donikkl from Germany, talks about the drink that goes so well with cookies: milk! Although most children won't be able to understand the German, they can talk about what they think

the song is about. The CD comes with an insert that describes each of the songs.

"Popcorn," from the recording *I'm a Rock Star,* **by Joanie Leeds and the Nightlights (Limbostar, 2010).**

Hop, snap, or clap along to corn as it pops.

"Shortnin' Bread," by Selloane, with Famoro Dioubaté, from the recording *Jazz Playground* **(Putumayo World Music, 2010).**

Selloane from South Africa and Guinea, performs a jazz version of "Shortnin' Bread."

"Spaghetti Legs," from the recording *Jim Gill Sings the Sneezing Song and Other Contagious Tunes,* **by Jim Gill (Jim Gill Music, 1993).**

Imagine that different body parts are turned into spaghetti noodles.

"Suppertime!" from the recording *A Family Album,* **by the Verve Pipe (LMNO Pop, 2009).**

This song has a lot of wordplay and asks why we call certain foods the names that we do. When you start to think about some of the foods and their names, they're quite silly. Ask children to think of other food names that are funny.

Swimming in Noodles, **by Jim Cosgrove (Jim Cosgrove, 2010).**

"Cool Daddy" has a Cajun flair and talks about two cool dads who cook food and help each other out. A silly song about noodles suggests that we all try some "Spaghetti and Goofballs." Who doesn't like chips and salsa? Celebrate this snack in "Chips and Salsa."

There's a Train . . ., **by We Kids Rock! (We Kids Rock, 2009).**

"Popcorn" is a jazzy song that describes the process of popping corn. Children can act out the song and pretend they are corn ready to pop. What happens to a meatball when someone sneezes? Find out the answer while listening to the rocking version of "On Top of Spaghetti."

"Victor Vito," from the recording *The Best of the Laurie Berkner Band,* **by the Laurie Berkner Band (Two Tomatoes Records, 2010).**

Find out what Victor and Freddie eat. Have children clap along to the rhythm.

"Why I Pack My Lunch," from the recording *My Name Is Chicken Joe,* **by Trout Fishing in America (Folle Avoine Productions, 2009).**

Trout Fishing in America sings about why packed lunches are better than school food and lists the wide variety of food found in the lunchroom. The food is indistinguishable, chewy, or crunchy when it's supposed to be the opposite. Some of the food includes rock-hard biscuits, snails, toenails, and snake. Eeww!

APPENDIX 1

GENERAL ACTION SONGS

Listed below is a sampling of action songs that you can teach children and then use when crowds are restless. Sometimes a little bit of music and movement is enough to help children refocus.

"Head, Shoulders, Knees and Toes," from the recording *Ladybug Music: Red Collection*, by Ladybug Music (Ladybug Music, 2009).
  The first time the song is sung in the traditional way. Each additional time, a word is left out and hummed so that by the end of the song almost all of it is hummed. The tempo of the song is brisk and the musical accompaniment sounds like Irish folk music. Children can do the motions with the song while trying to sing it and hum it at the same time.

"Hey, Dr. Knickerbocker," from the recording *Singing All the Way Home*, by Liz Buchanan (Antelope Dance Music, 2010).
  Each verse talks about keeping rhythm with different body parts from hips to fingers to knees to feet.

"Hokey Pokey," from the recording *Buckwheat Zydeco's Bayou Boogie*, by Buckwheat Zydeco (Musical Kidz, 2010).
  A Zydeco version of hokey pokey starts slow but increases in speed as the song progresses.

"Joe and the Button Factory," from the recording *Hot Peas 'N Butter, Volume 2: A Second Helping*, by Hot Peas 'N Butter (Hot Peas 'N Butter, 2010).
  The song starts with Joe doing one action, pushing a button. Each additional verse adds another action until Joe is pushing buttons with his knees, his elbows, his shoulders, and even his tongue.

"Jump, Jump," from the recording *I'm a Rock Star*, by Joanie Leeds and the Nightlights (Limbostar, 2010).
  Children can jump, shake, spin, and clap to this rock song.

"Let's Shake," by Dan Zanes and Friends, from the recording *Rock & Roll Playground* **(Putumayo World Music, 2010).**

Learn to dance the shake, the twist, the bug, and the hitchhike.

"Loop De Loop," from the recording *Ladybug Music: Purple Collection,* **by Ladybug Music (Ladybug Music, 2011).**

Follow the instructions and jump, clap, and dance along.

"Simon Says," from the recording *Everyone Loves to Dance!* **by Aaron Nigel Smith (Music for Little People, 2010).**

Listen closely and only follow the actions that Simon says.

"Them Bones," from the recording *Sing Along!* **by Caspar Babypants (Aurora Elephant Music, 2011).**

Pretend that you are a skeleton and dance around. Then point to the different bones as they are mentioned.

"Wake Up Hands," from the recording *There's a Train...,* **by We Kids Rock! (We Kids Rock, 2009).**

Start by waking up your hands, then your toes and arms.

APPENDIX 2

CROSS REFERENCE OF THEMED RESOURCES

This appendix includes a cross reference of books and songs that originated in one theme but also fit in another. For example, the books and songs listed below under Instrument Jam Band were originally in other chapters but also work as additional material for the instrument theme.

Instrument Jam Band
Books

- ▶ *The Django,* by Levi Pinfold (Templar Books, 2010).
- ▶ *Jake the Philharmonic Dog,* by Karen LeFrak and illustrated by Marcin Baranski (Walker and Company, 2006).
- ▶ *Knick Knack Paddy Whack,* by SteveSongs and illustrated by Christiane Engel (Barefoot Books, 2008).
- ▶ *One Shoe Blues, Starring B. B. King: Storybook, Song, Movie Short,* by Sandra Boynton (Workman Publishing, 2009).

Songs

- ▶ "More Cowbell," from the recording *I'm a Rock Star,* by Joanie Leeds and the Nightlights (Limbostar, 2010).
- ▶ "Syncopated Washboard Rhythm Song," from the recording *Banjo to Beatbox* by Cathy and Marcy with Christylez Bacon (Community Music, 2009).
- ▶ "What's That Sound?" from the recording *Make Your Own Someday: Silly Songs for the Shorter Set,* by The Jimmies (Pluckypea Publishing, 2006).

Feel the Rhythm
Books

- *Crash Bang Donkey!* by Jill Newton (Albert Whitman & Company, 2010).
- *Fritz Danced the Fandango,* by Alicia Potter and illustrated by Ethan Long (Scholastic Press, 2009).
- *There Was an Old Monster!* by Rebecca, Adrian, and Ed Emberley (Orchard Books, 2009).

Songs

- "The High-Low," from the recording *Radio Wayne,* by Wayne Brady (Walt Disney Records, 2011).
- "Me Mother Caught a Flea," from the recording *There's a Train...,* by We Kids Rock! (We Kids Rock, 2009).
- "We've Got Country in Our Body," from the recording *Kid's Country Song and Dance: Action, Sing-Along, Hoe-Down Fun!* by The Learning Station (Monopoli/The Learning Station, 2009).

Sing-Along Stories and Songs
Books

- *Cool Daddy Rat,* by Kristyn Crow and illustrated by Mike Lester (G. P. Putnam's Sons, 2008).
- *Fandango Stew,* by David Davis and illustrated by Ben Galbraith (Sterling, 2011).
- *The Middle-Child Blues,* by Kristyn Crow and illustrated by David Catrow (G. P. Putnam's Sons, 2009).
- *Rock 'N' Roll Mole,* by Carolyn Crimi and illustrated by Lynn Munsinger (Dial Books for Young Readers, 2011).

Songs

- "I Like Jazz," from the recording *I'm a Rock Star,* by Joanie Leeds and the Nightlights (Limbostar, 2010).
- "Oh Susanna," from the recording *Catch the Moon,* by Lisa Loeb and Elizabeth Mitchell (Sheridan Square Records, 2007).

▶ "You'll Sing a Song and I'll Sing a Song," from the recording *You'll Sing a Song and I'll Sing a Song,* by Ella Jenkins (Smithsonian/Folkways Records, 1989).

Moving and Grooving
Books

▶ *Abiyoyo,* by Pete Seeger and illustrated by Michael Hays (Simon & Schuster Books for Young Readers, 2001).
▶ *Clink,* by Kelly DiPucchio and illustrated by Matthew Myers (Balzer + Bray, 2011).
▶ *The Steel Pan Man of Harlem,* by Colin Bootman (Carolrhoda Books, 2009).

Songs

▶ "Like Never Before," from the recording *Oh Lucky Day!* by Lucky Diaz and the Family Jam Band (Rainy Day Dimes Music, 2011).
▶ "Monster Boogie," from the recording *Buzz Buzz,* by Laurie Berkner (Two Tomatoes Records, 1998).
▶ "Twist and Shout," from the recording *Buckwheat Zydeco's Bayou Boogie,* by Buckwheat Zydeco (Musical Kidz, 2010).

A Sound Hullabaloo
Books

▶ *Bedtime at the Swamp,* by Kristyn Crow and illustrated by Macky Pamintuan (HarperCollins, 2008).
▶ *Tortuga in Trouble,* by Ann Whitford Paul and illustrated by Ethan Long (Holiday House, 2009).

Songs

▶ "A Day at Camp Decibel," from the recording *Making Good Noise,* by Tom Chapin (Sundance Music, 2003).
▶ "Ratty Tat Tat," from the recording *There's a Train...,* by We Kids Rock! (We Kids Rock, 2009).

▶ "Spider-Man," by The Mr. T Experience, from the recording *Greasy Kid Stuff 3: Even More Songs from Inside the Radio* (Confidential Recordings, 2009).

Musical Potpourri
Books

▶ *The Carnival of the Animals,* with music by Camille Saint-Saëns, new verses by Jack Prelutsky and illustrated by Mary GrandPré (Alfred A. Knopf, 2010).
▶ *Hip & Hop, Don't Stop!* by Jef Czekaj (Disney Hyperion Books, 2010).
▶ *Pete the Cat: I Love My White Shoes,* by Eric Litwin and illustrated by James Dean (HarperCollins, 2010).
▶ *Thelonious Mouse,* by Orel Protopopescu and illustrated by Anne Wilsdorf (Farrar Straus Giroux, 2011).
▶ *When Louis Armstrong Taught Me Scat,* by Muriel Harris Weinstein and illustrated by R. Gregory Christie (Chronicle Books, 2008).

Songs

▶ "Earth Worm Disco," from the recording *Earth Worm Disco,* by Shira Kline (ShirLaLa, 2008).
▶ "Scat Like That," from the recording *Scat Like That: A Musical Word Odyssey,* by Cathy Fink and Marcy Marxer (Rounder Records, 2005).

Animal Antics
Books

▶ *The Talent Show,* by Jo Hodgkinson (Anderson Press USA, 2011).
▶ *Woof: A Love Story,* by Sarah Weeks and illustrated by Holly Berry (HarperCollins Children's Books, 2009).
▶ *ZooZical,* by Judy Sierra and illustrated by Marc Brown (Alfred A. Knopf, 2011).

Songs

▶ "Ants in Your Pants #99," from the recording *What a Ride!* by Eric Herman and the Invisible Band (Butter-Dog Records, 2009).

▶ "Do the Elephant," from the recording *Make Your Own Someday: Silly Songs for the Shorter Set,* by The Jimmies (Pluckypea Publishing, 2006).

▶ "I Know a Chicken," from the recording *The Best of the Laurie Berkner Band,* by The Laurie Berkner Band (Two Tomatoes Records, 2010).

▶ "Spanimals," from the recording *Make Your Own Someday: Silly Songs for the Shorter Set,* by The Jimmies (Pluckypea Publishing, 2006).

▶ "Two Little Blackbirds," from the recording *Ladybug Music: Yellow Collection,* by Ladybug Music (Ladybug Music, 2010).

Camp Do Re Mi
Books

▶ *The Great Monster Hunt,* by Norbert Landa and illustrated by Tim Warnes (Good Books, 2010).

▶ *The Haunted Hamburger and Other Ghostly Stories,* by David LaRochelle and illustrated by Paul Meisel (Dutton Children's Books, 2011).

▶ *Sipping Spiders Through a Straw: Campfire Songs for Monsters,* by Kelly DiPucchio and illustrated by Gris Grimly (Scholastic Press, 2008).

Songs

▶ "Bananas," from the recording *Jim Gill Presents Music Play for Folks of All Stripes* (Jim Gill Music, 2011).

▶ "Chewing Gum," from *Lisa Loeb's Silly Sing-Along: The Disappointing Pancake and Other Zany Songs,* by Lisa Loeb and illustrated by Ryan O'Rourke (Sterling Children's Books, 2011).

▶ "Joe and the Button Factory," from the recording *Hot Peas 'N Butter, Volume 2: A Second Helping,* by Hot Peas 'N Butter (Hot Peas 'N Butter, 2010).

Dragons, Monsters and Ghosts, Oh My!
Books

- ▶ *Boogie Knights,* by Lisa Wheeler and illustrated by Mark Siegel (Atheneum Books for Young Readers, 2008).
- ▶ *Dragon Pizzeria,* by Mary Morgan (Alfred A. Knopf, 2008).
- ▶ *Oscar and the Very Hungry Dragon,* by Ute Krause (North-South Books, 2010).

Song

- ▶ "Them Bones," from the recording *Sing Along!* by Caspar Babypants (Aurora Elephant Music, 2011).

Once Upon a Time
Books

- ▶ *The Gigantic Sweet Potato,* by Dianne de Las Casas and illustrated by Marita Gentry (Pelican Publishing Company, 2010).
- ▶ *Hans My Hedgehog: A Tale from the Brothers Grimm,* by Kate Coombs and illustrated by John Nickle (Atheneum Books for Young Readers, 2012).
- ▶ *The Runaway Wok,* by Ying Chang Compestine and illustrated by Sebastià Serra (Dutton Children's Books, 2011).

Songs

- ▶ "Hip-Hop Humpty Dumpty," from the recording *Banjo to Beatbox,* by Cathy and Marcy with Christylez Bacon (Community Music, 2009).
- ▶ "Little Lamb Jam," from the recording *Wake Up Clarinet!* by Oran Etkin (Oran Etkin's Timbalooloo, 2010).
- ▶ "Row, Row, Row Your Boat," performed by Charity and the JAMband, from the recording *Rock & Roll Playground* (Putumayo World Music, 2010).

Earth Celebration
Books

▶ *Jo MacDonald Saw a Pond,* by Mary Quattlebaum and illustrated by Laura J. Bryant (Dawn Publications, 2011).

▶ *The Rainforest Grew All Around,* by Susan K. Mitchell and illustrated by Connie McLennan (Sylvan Dell Publishing, 2007).

▶ *Way Up in the Arctic,* by Jennifer Ward and illustrated by Kenneth J. Spengler (Rising Moon, 2007).

Songs

▶ "Animal Adventure," from the recording *The Animal Faire,* by Tony Robinson (Tony Robinson Music, 2011).

▶ "Free Little Bird," from the recording *Catch the Moon,* by Lisa Loeb and Elizabeth Mitchell (Sheridan Square Records, 2007).

▶ "I Love the Mountains," from the recording *Let's Go! Travel, Camp and Car Songs,* by Susie Tallman and Friends (Rock Me Baby Records, 2007).

Game Time
Book

▶ *How Do You Wokka-Wokka?* by Elizabeth Bluemle and illustrated by Randy Cecil (Candlewick Press, 2009).

Songs

▶ "Head, Shoulders, Knees and Toes," from the recording *Ladybug Music: Red Collection,* by Ladybug Music (Ladybug Music, 2009).

▶ "Hokey Pokey," from the recording *Buckwheat Zydeco's Bayou Boogie,* by Buckwheat Zydeco (Musical Kidz, 2010).

▶ "Shimmy Shimmy Coco Pop," from the recording *Ladybug Music: Pink Collection,* by Ladybug Music (Ladybug Music, 2011).

Tasty Tunes and Tales
Books

- ▶ *Bad Boys Get Cookie!* by Margie Palatini and illustrated by Henry Cole (Katherine Tegen Books, 2006).
- ▶ *The Gingerbread Girl Goes Animal Crackers,* by Lisa Campbell Ernst (Dutton Children's Books, 2011).
- ▶ *The Library Gingerbread Man,* by Dotti Enderle and illustrated by Colleen M. Madden (Upstart Books, 2010).
- ▶ *Marsupial Sue Presents "The Runaway Pancake,"* by John Lithgow and illustrated by Jack E. Davis (Simon & Schuster Books for Young Readers, 2005).

Songs

- ▶ "Gorilla Song," performed by Sha Na Na, from *Blue Moo: 17 Jukebox Hits From Way Back Never,* by Sandra Boynton (Workman Publishing, 2007).
- ▶ "Muffin Man," from the recording *Rock All Day Rock All Night,* by The Nields (Mercy House Productions, 2008).
- ▶ "Pots and Pans," by the Bacon Brothers, from *Dog Train: Deluxe Illustrated Lyrics Book of the Unpredictable Rock-And-Roll Journey,* by Sandra Boynton (Workman Publishing, 2005).

INDEX

M